Continued Success

401(k) Sales Champion™

A Guide For Financial Sales Professionals To Acquire And Retain 401(k) Plans

by: Christopher H. Barlow and Stephen D. Wilt

First Edition

KNOWHOW LLC 401 k

EMPOWERING FINANCIAL SALES PROFESSIONALS

P.O. Box 90102
Dayton, OH 45490

Published by:
Knowhow 401(k), LLC.
P.O. Box 90102
Dayton, OH 45490

401(k) Sales Champion™: A Guide For Financial Sales Professionals To
Acquire And Retain 401(k) Plans.

Book design and layout developed by:
Maddox Marketing Group, Inc., Akron, OH

02 01 00   1 2 3 4 5 6 7 8 9

Printed in the United States of America

International Standard Book Number: 0-9704950-0-5
Library of Congress Number:

401(k) Sales Champion™

Dedication

I want to first of all express my love and gratitude toward my wife who encouraged me to pursue this very satisfying endeavor. My thanks also goes out to my daughters, who without any encouragement, help me to stay focused on what is really important.

Finally, I would like to thank all of the sales champions, especially Mr. Kevin Shepard, who have taught me more about servicing the 401(k) market than any other resource. Continued great health my friend.

– Chris Barlow

To Holly, the kindest, most giving and loving wife a man could imagine. You bring joy to my life every day and your love inspires me.

– Steve Wilt

Chapter / Question and Discussion Index

Chapter 1: Do You Want To Be A 401(k) Sales Champion™?

Questions and Discussions   **Page#**

What are the characteristics of 401(k) Sales Champions™?   5

Get paid 52 times per year!   11

Incubation of Future Clients   14

Chapter 2: Preparation: Enhancing Your 401(k) Knowledge

What makes a sucessful 401(k) plan?   19

The 401(k) market is commoditized   21

The anatomy of a 401(k) plan   23

Should you develop a technical understanding of 401(k) plans?   30

Chapter 3: Preparation: Developing A 401(k) Sales Champion™ Practice

How do you build a 401(k) practice?   31

What resources are available to help you accomplish your professional goals for servicing the 401(k) marketplace?   32

Why do employers (plan sponsors) adopt 401(k) plans?   32

What does a plan sponsor expect from you, the financial sales professional?   33

How do you reinforce to plan sponsors and plan participants that you are the financial sales professional they should choose?   39

How do you build your reputation as an expert?   42

Team selling and services – Bringing expertise together to win   43

How do you build your team?   44

Should you represent several 401(k) vendor programs?   45

What are the benefits for you to be consultative and recommend the best 401(k) program you can?   46

What are the expenses for an employer to establish and maintain a 401(k) plan?   48

What are the costs of establishing a 401(k) plan?   51

What are trustees' fiduciary responsibilities?   53

Not one, but two ways to construct a 401(k) plan   56

Bundled or unbundled? – How to know which 401(k) program is
    best for your plan sponsor   57
Daily valuation vs. balance forward record keeping – Which is
    better for your plan sponsors?   59

Chapter 4: Planning: Increasing Your Probability Of Success

A business plan is essential   61
Level One Activity – Creating Your Mission Statement   62
Level One Activity – Documenting Your Goals   63
Level One Activity – Establish 401(k) Practice Structure   64
Why should you partner for 401(k) plans?   65
Is a regional/national/international team viable   67
Level Two Activities – Bringing Your Business Plan to Life   67

Chapter 5: Planning: Establishing Vendor Partnerships – Which 401(k) Vendor(s) Will You Represent?

Who is the 401(k) vendor wholesaler?   69
What are the qualities that employers look for in a 401(k)
    vendor(s) program?   69
What should you know about the 401(k) vendor(s) program?   71
How do you decide which 401(k) vendors programs to represent?   74
How can the 401(k) vendor(s) wholesaler help you to acquire
    and retain 401(k) plans?   76

Chapter 6: Prospecting: Determining With Whom You Want To Do Business

What is the key to 401(k) prospecting success?   79
What is the prospecting process?   79
Where should you look for prospects?   85
What are some non-traditional prospecting ideas?   86
How do you build and manage a database?   87
How do you overcome objections from the "gatekeeper"
    receptionist as you attempt to initially verify lead information?   89

When is the best time of year to begin contacting prospective
    401(k) plan decision-makers?   89
Is there a better market time –up, down or side-ways– to prospect
    for 401(k) plans?   90
Who at the prospect company should you contact first?   91

Chapter 7: Profiling: Discovering What You Need To Know In Order To Win The 401(k) Plan

How do you open the initial call to the 401(k) decision-maker?   93
How do you qualify a 401(k) plan prospect and what are the most
    applicable profiling questions to ask during the initial contact?   96
What are some appropriate questions to ask a decision-maker
    who is just starting a 401(k) at his company?   97
How do you respond to questions from the 401(k) decision-makers?   97
What are common 401(k) start-up plan objections?   99
What do you do when the call is going nowhere?   99
What is the progression of a 401(k) plan prospect?   100
How do you manage the time between initial contact and the
    discovery meeting with a prospect?   101
Demonstrate your quality service standards during the prospecting
    process   102
What is the purpose of the discovery meeting with a 401(k)
    plan sponsor?   102
How should you conduct the discovery meeting?   103
What profiling questions do you ask during the discovery meeting?   105
What should you listen for during the discovery meeting?   107
How can you respond to a 401(k) plan decision-maker when they
    state, "As a result of poor service from the current 401(k) plan
    vendor, participation in the 401(k) plan is declining?"   108
What should you promise your 401(k) plan decision-maker prospects?   108

Chapter 8: Presenting Solutions: Effectively Communicating Your Value And Solutions

What is the proposal process?   109
How do you work with 401(k) plan search consultants?   110

What is a Request For Proposal (RFP)?   111

How do you build your 401(k) sales presentation?   112

Who will you present to?   112

What should you present during the sales presentation?   113

What should you say during the sales presentation?   114

How do you open your sales presentation?   116

How can you use comparative matrixes during the sales presentation?   117

How do you conduct a sales presentation to the plan participants?   118

What should the 401(k) vendor wholesaler and/or other 401(k)
     vendor representatives present?   119

What should you listen for during the sales presentation?   119

How should you respond to questions and/or objections by the
     decision-makers?   120

When should you go for the close?   120

What are some effective follow-up techniques to the 401(k) plan
     decision-makers after the sales presentation?   122

How do you manage the time between proposals and closing the sale?   123

Chapter 9: Implementation Of Service: Positively Beginning The Relationship

What do you do when you win the 401(k) plan?   127

What occurs operationally during a conversation?   128

What are the basic musts for a "welcome" conference call?   131

What are the various types of employee retirement education meetings?   131

Who at the company should be involved with the development
     of employee retirement education events?   132

When should you schedule enrollment meetings?   133

Is there any difference in the enrollment meeting between a
     start-up and a conversion plan?   134

Selling a 401(k) plan to employees.   134

What should you not talk about during the enrollment meeting?   137

What are some questions most often asked by employees during
     the enrollment meeting?   137

Why are off-site educational events effective?   138

How do you conduct employee education events at remote
     company locations?   139

Chapter 10: Ongoing Service: Retaining The Relationship

How do you retain your 401(k) plans? 141

Why is ongoing service important? 142

How do you manage your time as your practice grows? 142

What do you talk about at ongoing employee retirement education meetings? 143

How can you develop cross-selling strategies for the plan sponsor and plan participants? 144

How can you assist plan participants and build relationships with them? 145

What are other ways of staying in front of plan participants? 146

How does an employer evaluate investment performance? 147

What are written investment policies? 148

How does a plan sponsors evaluate the effectiveness of the total 401(k) program? 149

How do you help employers manage their fiduciary responsibilities? 149

Chapter 11: Selected Topics

What should you do when you inherit a plan from a colleague? 153

How do you acquire 401(k) plans as a result of a broker-of-record change? 153

How do you work with an employer that does not prefer an ideal 401(k) plan? 154

What if the plan sponsor does not select you? 154

What does the future hold for 401(k) plans? 156

Introduction

How many people have told you that they are looking forward to retirement? The fact of the matter is, if we were able to, the majority of us would stop working and start living the good life NOW! Oh, if only we could be sure we would be living the good life.

Retirees are living longer. On average, a retiree will spend as many years in retirement as they did working. The biggest factor in determining how well they live will be, in large part, dependent on how well they take advantage of tax-deferred savings options like 401(k) plans.

You, as a financial sales professional, have an unprecedented opportunity to guide and counsel thousands of Americans in preparing for the retirement they've dreamed of, as a 401(k) Sales Champion™.

Having serviced the 401(k) marketplace for a combined 30 years, our rewards have been numerous. We believe that by writing this book, our rewards will continue to multiply. Our contributions to 401(k) Sales Champion™ - A Guide for Financial Sales Professionals to Acquire and Retain 401(k) Plans have come as a result of countless hours spent "smiling and dialing," profiling, and presenting and servicing to thousands of 401(k) plans.

You will find in the following eleven chapters nearly 100 items of discussion, as well as, nearly 100 actionable ideas to enhance your 401(k) knowledge and ability to prospect, sell and service 401(k) plans.

In 2001, the 401(k) plan will celebrate its 20th anniversary. Still in its infancy, there are far more 401(k) plans and plan participants to be serviced than 401(k) Sales Champions™ to service them. Your opportunity is clear, join in!

A 401(k) Sales Champion™ is a financial sales professional who has developed expertise in the acquisition and retention of 401(k) plans by delivering value-added service to assist the plan sponsor and plan participants. The 401(k) Sales Champion™ is thus poised to capitalize on the unprecedented opportunity that the 401(k) market offers.

Many financial sales professionals want to service the 401(k) market, however, most fail to realize the competitive nature of the market, the time required to complete the sales cycle, and the knowledge-base they need to possess to be a true 401(k) Sales Champion™.

The genesis of 401(k) plans began with the enactment of the Tax Reform Act of 1978 under section 401, paragraph k, Congress authorized the creation of Cash or Deferred Arrangements (CODA). In the spring of 1981, the IRS gave provisional approval to the first 401(k) plan, created by a benefits consultant named R. Theodore Benna, "the father of 401(k) plans". The plan submitted by Benna and his partner offered many of the features present in today's plans, including pre-tax salary reduction and employer-matching contributions.

In 1981, the institutional retirement plan marketplace was comprised of for-profit and not-for-profit organizations, using both defined benefit and defined contribution plans where services were dominated by banks and insurance companies. It would not be until the late 1980s that a third major competitor would emerge to dominate the 401(k) marketplace; the mutual fund companies.

When speaking to an employer who might not understand the difference between the two types of corporate qualified retirement plans, this is a way to help them understand:

Defined Benefit
Known: The benefit at retirement
Unknown: The amount of annual contribution

Defined Contribution
Known: The amount of annual contribution
Unknown: The benefit at retirement

"More employees participate in 401(k) and other defined contribution plans than in defined benefit plans, according to the Department of Labor. And defined contribution assets are expected to grow at a 12.5% rate over the next five years, according to Spectrem Group, a consulting and research firm based in San Francisco.

Source: CFO Magazine, October 1998, "Online Lifeline," Jeannie Mandelker.

October 19, 1987 was a day of great change, not only for the account balances of the investing public, but also for the competitive forces in the 401(k) market. Courageous 401(k) plan participants eager to capitalize on depressed mutual fund prices with traditional balance forward recordkeeping systems found that their orders placed in October did not execute until the end of the fourth quarter. A cry went out for a more responsive account information and reallocation system by plan participants and daily valuation gained momentum.

Do you want to be a 401(k) Sales Champion™?

Daily Valuation recordkeeping systems, which were predominately supplied by mutual fund companies, became more and more popular. And today, the Top 10 list of 401(k) vendors is comprised of mutual fund companies and vendors who use mutual funds as investment offerings for their clients. **The power shift amongst 401(k) vendors was driven from a service perspective instead of an investment performance or fee issues –a great lesson to always remember as you compete for 401(k) plans.**

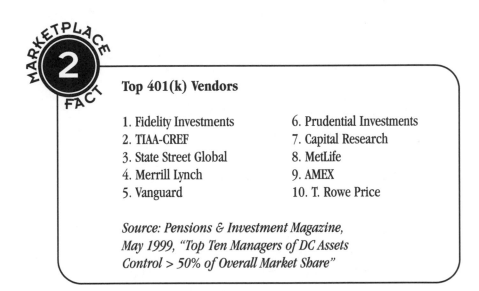

MARKETPLACE FACT 2

Top 401(k) Vendors

1. Fidelity Investments	6. Prudential Investments
2. TIAA-CREF	7. Capital Research
3. State Street Global	8. MetLife
4. Merrill Lynch	9. AMEX
5. Vanguard	10. T. Rowe Price

Source: Pensions & Investment Magazine, May 1999, "Top Ten Managers of DC Assets Control > 50% of Overall Market Share"

Most financial sales professionals start and quickly stop prospecting for 401(k) plans because of unrealistic expectations. There certainly is a larger universe of individual prospects than institutional 401(k) plans. The lead-time and the distance between successes are greater in acquiring 401(k) plans than individual clients. Most 401(k) plans are either created or change 401(k) vendors on a calendar quarter, and the decision process can be long and tedious. A three to nine month period is the norm from first contact to final decision, assuming you are prospecting a motivated employer.

With a longer sale time and a smaller universe of potential customers, you must be capable of managing your time efficiently, balancing prospecting with servicing existing clients. Though success in the

401(k) Sales Champion™

401(k) business requires a long-term commitment, the payoff can be enormous with opportunities to convert plan participants and business owners to individual clients as well.

Many financial sales professionals manage 401(k) plans but few are 401(k) Sales Champions™. Whether your goal is to make 401(k) plan management a small part of your practice, or you want to specialize in the market, the seven activities of acquiring and retaining 401(k) plans are applicable.

The seven activities for acquiring and retaining 401(k) plans are:

1 **Preparation:** Enhancing your 401(k) knowledge

2 **Planning:** Increasing your probability of success

3 **Prospecting:** Determining with whom you want to do business

4 **Profiling:** Uncovering what you need to know in order to win the 401(k) plan

5 **Presenting Solutions:** Effectively communicating your value and solutions

6 **Implementation Service:** Positively beginning the relationship

7 **Ongoing Service:** Retaining the relationship

When a 401(k) Sales Champion™ communicates value to prospective plan sponsors, they tell the plan sponsor that they specialize in the 401(k) market. By saying this, he or she exudes confidence and competency, which has tremendous impact on the judgment of prospective plan sponsors. If you are passionate about the 401(k) market and learn it inside and out, you will become a successful 401(k) Sales Champion™. Focus on representing an optimal 401(k) program, delivering exceptional services to plan sponsors and, most importantly, plan participants.

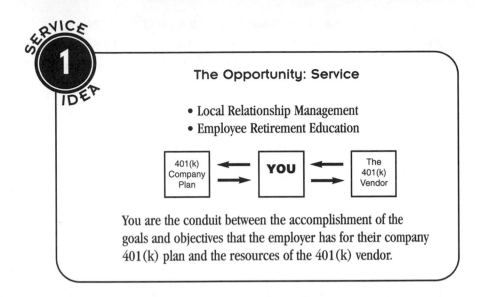

The Opportunity: Service

- Local Relationship Management
- Employee Retirement Education

401(k) Company Plan ⟷ **YOU** ⟷ The 401(k) Vendor

You are the conduit between the accomplishment of the goals and objectives that the employer has for their company 401(k) plan and the resources of the 401(k) vendor.

401(k) Sales Champions™ deliver exceptional local support by being the relationship manager for the employer with the 401(k) vendor as well as serving as the employees' Retirement Coach™. 401(k) Sales Champions™ are often part of a team of financial sales professionals, and they are recognized in their communities as 401(k) experts.

Most 401(k) Sales Champions™ did not begin their sales careers with a specific focus on selling 401(k) plans. More times than not they were asked by an individual client if they could help with their company 401(k) plan, and that is how they got their start in 401(k) sales. 401(k) plans are the primary focus for a 401(k) Sales Champion™.

What are the characteristics of a 401(k) Sales Champion ™?

A 401(k) Sales Champion™ consistently demonstrates an array of characteristics that attract and aid in the retention of 401(k) clients.

Trusted consultant
Helping the plan sponsor and plan participants to make the best decisions while delivering proactive local relationship management and employee retirement education services.

401(k) Sales Champion™

A reputation in their community as an expert

What a 401(k) Sales Champion™ will tell you is, "**401(k) plan sponsors do not buy a 401(k) program from a 401(k) vendor; 401(k) plan sponsors buy a 401(k) vendor program from me.**"

Excellent communicators

Effective communications between you, the 401(k) vendor, the plan sponsor, and plan participants are vital to the success of all partners in the 401(k) plan.

A "bulldog" mentality

They make sure that if their plan sponsor or plan participant client has an issue with the 401(k) vendor, the issue is resolved quickly. The 401(k) Sales Champion™ is the one who picks up the phone and calls the 401(k) vendor, relieving the plan sponsor or plan participant from following up with the vendor to make sure the issue is resolved.

The passion of a teacher and/or coach for helping the plan participants

After all, part of their role is to empower employees to establish and maintain healthy savings habits and educate employees about the importance of managing the single largest pool of money they will likely accumulate in their lives.

One day, you may find yourself in a hot, dirty, crowded factory attempting to educate a group of employees who have little knowledge of the investment management topics you are about to explain. As you are speaking louder to overcome the hum of the machines, to steal a line from a popular Talking Heads song, "You may ask yourself, what am I doing here?" If you do your best, you are likely to positively change the lives of every person in attendance. At this point you are not a typical financial sales professional. You are not singularly managing assets for high-net-worth individuals. Instead, you are also providing life-changing advice to hard-working Americans. The average 401(k) plan participant will more likely admit that they know little about investing and that they need your help.

6

Over the years, upon return visits to the plan participants, they will thank you. You will find plan participants who have accumulated hundreds of thousands of dollars in their 401(k) account. They may build a house, send a child to college and hopefully retire more comfortably because of you.

Not only will 401(k) Sales Champions™ experience gratification knowing they can impact the future of plan participants, but they will also gain cross-selling opportunities and acquire future business by building rapport with the plan sponsor and the plan participants.

Here are other important factors that can determine a 401(k) Sales Champion's™ success in the 401(k) marketplace:

Length of Service
Very few 401(k) Sales Champions™ started their careers in financial sales focusing exclusively on servicing the 401(k) marketplace. The lead-time in acquiring a 401(k) plan can be as short as three months and as long as nine months, assuming that you are prospecting a motivated employer. If a relationship is present, the lead-time can be shorter. Length of service in the financial services industry is less important when acquiring 401(k) plans if you have experience in a particular field that enhances your ability to gain and work with clients. For example, we know a financial sales professional who owned an in-home nursing care business. Through this endeavor, he cultivated a strong network of business owners and executives. When he entered the 401(k) marketplace, he tapped into his network and used his knowledge of these prospective clients' businesses and their employees' needs. By capitalizing on his network base and communicating the value of a well-managed 401(k) plan, he quickly built a client base and became a 401(k) Sales Champion™.

New financial sales professionals may have production or asset gathering goals required by their respective employers. New financial sales professionals should focus their energy and time on meeting management's objectives. **Usually, it is wise for the "rookie" broker to follow his employer's activity and production guidelines. After**

401(k) Sales Champion™

all, employers base their training and sales goals on the best practices of top producers.

Whether you are a new or a tenured financial sales professional, you need to efficiently manage the time you dedicate toward prospecting for and servicing 401(k) plans.

Make-up of current book of business
Current individual clients who are decision-makers (such as CEOs, CFOs, owners, presidents, etc.) and other influential employees at companies can help you gain a 401(k) plan. Networking with business executives can only strengthen your chances for developing relationships that lead to 401(k) plan victories.

Attitude
Plan sponsors ask themselves questions about you; "Do I trust this person?", " Do I believe this person?", "Will they be able to communicate with my employees?" A successful 401(k) Sales Champion™ communicates and demonstrates that he is genuinely concerned about the plan participants. He encourages the plan participants to understand that the 401(k) plan is a tool their employer has provided –a tool that can help the plan participant accumulate and manage their retirement wealth. He arranges one-on-one meetings with all employees to make sure that they understand how to best use the 401(k) to accomplish their personnel objectives.

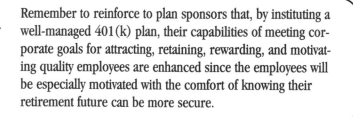

Remember to reinforce to plan sponsors that, by instituting a well-managed 401(k) plan, their capabilities of meeting corporate goals for attracting, retaining, rewarding, and motivating quality employees are enhanced since the employees will be especially motivated with the comfort of knowing their retirement future can be more secure.

Do you want to be a 401(k) Sales Champion™?

Creativity

A 401(k) Sales Champion™ will do things that others do not to attract prospective plan sponsors and to promote the 401(k) plan among the employees.

One 401(k) Sales Champion™ we know conducts an annual event, inviting all current and prospective plan sponsors, plan participants and their guests. The event is used to inform the attendees about changes and trends in the 401(k) marketplace as well as other related and unrelated topics that are of interest to participants. There are exhibits on gardening, cooking and home decorating. Attendees leave the event feeling great about the 401(k) Sales Champion™ because he has demonstrated interest in more than their company 401(k) plan.

The 401(k) opportunity

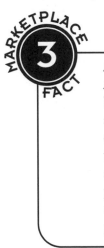

According to R. Theodore Benna, founder of The 401(k) Association, the future of 401(k) plans is bright. The number of these plans is expected to continue growing in the short term, especially among companies with fewer than 100 employees and workers at non-profit organizations. Long-term results, Benna believes, will be influenced by regulatory action in Washington D.C. and law changes that could allow participants who move from one employer's 401(k) plan to another to be immediately eligible to join the new employer's plan.

According to plans participating in the survey, 82.5% of eligible employees held balances in their 401(k) plans.

Source: Profit Sharing/401(k) Council of America 43rd Annual Survey of Profit Sharing and 401(k) plans for 1999 plan year.

New plan formations –especially among smaller firms –is one reason for the rapid growth in the 401(k) marketplace. Increasing wages, a growing awareness of the need for retirement savings and more than 75 million Baby Boomers reaching the pre-retirement age group are other factors contributing to the growth of the 401(k) market. January 1, 2006 will mark the 25th anniversary of the 401(k) plan. By this time, Benna claims the number of 401(k) plans will likely triple and assets could exceed $2 trillion.

27 million workers have saved more than $1 trillion in 401(k) plans, and the average account balance now stands at $40,000. At least 10% of participants have amassed more than $100,000.

Source: Money.com "Get the MAX from your 401(k), Penelope Wang, June 28, 2000.

These numbers are conservative. 401(k) plan assets grow rapidly. Employers want to create 401(k) programs to enhance their business in the eyes of their existing valuable employees and also make their firm attractive to talented prospective employees. 401(k) plans are an important tool for employers to attract, retain, reward, and motivate quality employees who help determine the company's bottom line.

Given the potential for growth in the 401(k) plan market, it is interesting to note that today **there are more 401(k) plans than 401(k) Sales Champions™**. There are few financial sales professionals who understand how or want to service the 401(k) marketplace. Even fewer

Do you want to be a 401(k) Sales Champion™?

are committed to offering dedicated service to the plan sponsor and the plan participants. Most financial sales professionals will not be willing to invest enough time to provide the necessary service to plan sponsors and plan participants. Many are not interested in getting their "hands dirty" in employee enrollment sessions or annual trustee meetings. This is good news for you. Once you build a reputation for genuine quality service, you can write your ticket to success and prosperity in the 401(k) marketplace.

When you service the 401(k) market, your career will change for the better in many ways. In time, your book of individual clients will include a group of business owners, company executives and motivated savers.

Servicing the 401(k) market offers several personal and financial rewards to financial sales professionals. Benefits include:
- **The ability to annuitize commissions**
- **Incubate future clients**
- **Create referral and cross-selling opportunities**
- **The creation of quality business**

Get paid 52 times a year!

As financial sales professionals, we all hope to build our business and annuitize our income by providing excellent investment management service to our customers. With 401(k) plans, you will counsel and service the plan sponsor and the plan participants, helping them to accomplish their respective goals for the 401(k) plan. We also want to have "deep" business relationships with our clients. 401(k) plans help create the rapport necessary with plan sponsors and plan participants to enhance cross-selling opportunities. Client retention creates greater production and, therefore, your income potential.

401(k) Sales Champion™

SALES 1 IDEA

A great 401(k) relationship will grow into other business. Once you are in the door, the service you provide will lend itself to other opportunities. We have seen 401(k) plan relationships grow into pensions, life insurance, business lines of credit, business cash management, deferred compensation plans, and the development of individual client business.

Servicing the 401(k) market can send your business into hyperspace. As the illustration below shows, the financial reward to those who successfully service the 401(k) market is great. For example, say over a five-year period you acquire ten 401(k) plans, each having an average of 300 participants and $10 million in plan assets. Further, the plan assets are invested in mutual funds, which pay an average of 1% in up-front commissions, a 1% pay-out on deposits and a 25 basis point annual trail, you have a business that provides initial –and most importantly –long-term monetary benefits.

Assumptions:

- Two new company 401(k) plans added each year for the next 5 years
- Number of total eligible employees added each year - 600
- 80% participation among eligible employees in each year
- Average annual participant compensation - $35,000
- 6% average participant contribution percentage
- Employer match of 25¢ on the $1 up to the first 6% saved by the plan participant
- 1% commission paid on takeover assets and new contributions
- Annual 25bp "trailer" commission paid on all assets
- 10% average annual growth of plan assets due to investment activity

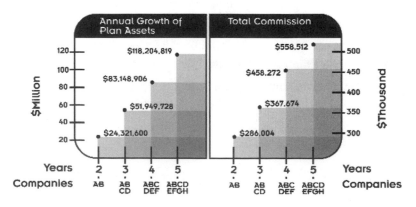

Do you want to be a 401(k) Sales Champion™?

By the end of the fifth year you could generate more than $558,000 in commissions, accumulate more than $118 million in assets and have more than 2,400 people saving for their retirement with you. You can also look forward to the opportunity to gather additional commissions from cross-selling opportunities. By successfully servicing the 401(k) market, you will create a business, which will consistently give you an opportunity to provide supplemental financial services to plan participants. We cannot emphasize this point enough. **The most significant benefit of servicing the 401(k) market is in the long term.** You will not only receive regular payments to service your 401(k) customers, but you will also begin to handle the needs of plan participants who you have incubated into priority clients.

Each payday at a company with a 401(k) that you manage is a payday for you. If you want a steady stream of income –cash flow that can be counted on –the 401(k) market is ideal. After all, even when the economy struggles, contributions to 401(k) plans are typically unaffected.

The 401(k) market is a great annuitized business for financial sales professionals because it offers an ongoing flow of income and assets. 401(k) plan participants designate a pre-tax percentage of their income to be deducted from their paychecks. The plan sponsors can then match the participant's contribution, perhaps add profit-sharing dollars, and the commissions for all dollars contributed are on their way to you. As contributions continue, you continue to get paid. As the number of 401(k) plans you manage increases, you can literally have millions of dollars invested each month, generating thousands of dollars in current contribution and mutual fund trailer commissions.

Trailer commissions are typically .25 basis points and are paid on mutual funds based on accumulated assets. For example, if you have $100 million in mutual funds in your 401(k) plans, on a quarterly basis you will earn $62,500 in trailer commissions. As the plan assets grow through contributions and appreciation, the mutual fund trailer commissions grow, continually increasing your compensation. Managing 401(k) plans is an ideal way to annuitize your commission potential

401(k) Sales Champion™

and simultaneously grow your business.

Since servicing 401(k) plans allows you to annuitize your production and asset growth, you will have more time to gather new accounts and develop new individual client relationships outside of your 401(k) business. This combination of annuitized business from 401(k) plans and freedom for additional account growth will stimulate your career for years to come.

Incubation of Future Clients

401(k) plans "incubate" your future clientele. How? By providing the structure necessary for the plan participants to build wealth. Along with regular commissions to service your 401(k) plans, you will also begin to service the needs of plan participants and plan sponsors who want to take full advantage of the wealth building and preservation products you can offer.

As financial sales professionals, we want to have a steady stream of new customers to grow our income. Perhaps one day all 401(k) plans will allow a plan participant to manage their 401(k) account balance with their choice of financial service company and financial sales professional. This is another reason to **acquire these plans while they are group situations, with the opportunity to build individual relationships with the plan participants.**

When you enter the 401(k) marketplace and gain those first plans, it is important to remember who you are helping and cater to their needs.

> **There are four categories of potential client groups to serve when you win a 401(k):**
>
> 1. **The Business:** You can sell additional products like buy/sell insurance, lines of credit and cash management products.
>
> 2. **Business Owners:** They have personal financial planning

Do you want to be a 401(k) Sales Champion™?

concerns such as an estate, business succession, deferred compensation, and college funding for their children, grandchildren and often large, separate investment portfolios.

3. The Employees: They have a multitude of potential financial planning issues, in addition to their retirement saving needs.

4. Referrals: You receive these from satisfied decision-makers, centers of influence and plan participants.

MARKETPLACE **6** FACT

36% of participants use a financial sales professional as a source of information for their 401(k) plan investment decisions.

32% use a Stock Broker
18% use an Insurance Agent/Broker
15% use a Mutual Fund Representative
8% use a Bank Investment Representative
8% use an Independent Financial Planner
19% we're not sure or stated another choice

Source: Spectrum Group/Access Research, 1997

Cross-selling and Referral Opportunities

When you service the 401(k) market, keep in mind that you have been anointed by someone employees hold close to their heart, at least every payday; their employer. You have been granted instant credibility. **Every employee meeting is a potential seminar sale.** At your disposal is an audience of willing investors that have given you detailed personal financial information. You have a captive group of people to build cross-selling opportunities. **Remember if you acquire a 100-participant 401(k) program, it could take more than a year to acquire the same number of individual clients through traditional means.**

SERVICE 3 IDEA

Company management and other generously compensated employees are the easiest group of employees to cross-sell. You will have contact with them through the 401(k) committee or board meetings. It is as simple as asking, "Is there anything I can do for you on an individual basis?" Then just listen and let them tell you everything. Your regular presence at the company will win you business. Stop by executives' offices and ask if they have any questions. You will be amazed how they will stop what they are doing to talk about their money. Higher paid employees will want to set follow-up appointments at their office. Perhaps the company will pay for their executives to receive a complete financial plan as an extra employee benefit program for the management group.

SERVICE 4 IDEA

Be patient in your cross-selling of plan participants. Assume that the plan decision-makers have been told by your competition that you will actively prospect their employees. You need to assure the plan decision-makers right away that this is not the case. Tell them you are able to assist their employees with their future financial needs, however, you will not actually prospect them.

Explain, "The reality, Mr./Mrs. Decision-Maker, is that your employees will gravitate toward me. As I am here consistently holding education meetings and promoting the plan, your employees will ask for my help. I will also help those participants who fall below my minimum account size criteria, because they are a part of your plan."

By successfully working the 401(k) market, you will create a business, which will consistently provide you an opportunity to offer additional financial products to plan participants. Tapping into the individual investor market is more challenging than it once was. You not only have peer financial sales professionals to compete against; you also have

Do you want to be a 401(k) Sales Champion™?

other potential obstacles that stand between you and a prospective client, including the Internet, Caller ID and dwindling response rates to direct mail pieces. Some financial sales professionals cannot afford to pursue the individual investor as they did in previous years because of the increase in non-traditional competition.

All financial sales professionals who want to build a 401(k) practice into their book of business need to memorize and recite this phrase to deliver to 401(k) plan decision-maker prospects, or individual clients who know a 401(k) plan decision-maker:

"The next time you look to enhance the company 401(k) plan, I would like to have an opportunity to compete."

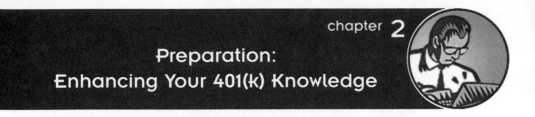

chapter 2

Preparation:
Enhancing Your 401(k) Knowledge

What makes a successful 401(k) Plan?

Successful 401(k) plans are understood and managed as a partnership between the employer, employees, 401(k) program vendor, and you the financial sales professional. Each partner has particular objectives and goals they hope to accomplish by participating with the company 401(k) plan. The best run 401(k) programs are those where all partners understand their objectives, roles and responsibilities as well as those of the other partners. Here is a list of 401(k) plan partners and their objectives:

Employer/Plan Sponsor
Objective: They want to attract, retain, reward and motivate quality, productive employees in order to maintain and increase profitability. In addition, they want to build retirement wealth for themselves.

Employee/Plan Participant
Objective: They want to confidently accumulate and manage their retirement wealth.

401(k) Vendor(s)
Objective: They want to build an ever-expanding stream of ongoing management fees as well as foster relationships with financial sales professionals, plan participants, employers, and referrals from all.

Financial Sales Professional
Objective: You want to generate an ongoing commission stream, gather assets and build relationships which could lead to additional business.

401(k) Sales Champion™

The ideal 401(k) program scenario happens when all partners combine their focused energy, resources, experience, and wisdom to create an optimal environment from which all partners can accomplish their respective goals.

A survey conducted by the Employee Benefit Institute, the American Savings Education Council and Matthew Greenwald & Associates, for Columbus, Ohio-based Nationwide Financial found that small-business owners who offer retirement plans report a positive impact on their ability to attract and retain workers.

Source: Business First of Columbus, May 29, 2000, "Firms with better benefits have more profitable results."

Since a 401(k) plan for an employer is an employee benefit "tool" used to attract, retain, reward, and motivate quality, productive employees, you become an extension of the company human resources department. **By communicating and demonstrating your ability and desire to better help employees use the 401(k) "tool," you will help the employer/plan sponsor accomplish their corporate goals of attracting, retaining, rewarding, and motivating quality, productive employees.**

If the employees are confident with the company 401(k) plan, they will have another reason to buy-in to being employed at the company. You will hear some employees say that they distrust their employer and they are concerned about what is really happening to their money. These employees have an incorrect perception that you can correct. Knowing that the employees' money is held in a trust account, separated from their employers and that they can check an "800" number or the Internet to make sure their contributions were deposited, gives you the ability to promote trust between the employee and their employer.

Plan sponsors and committee members who choose the company

401(k) program vendor are becoming more knowledgeable about the legal and technical aspects of 401(k) plans through experience. You should have a comfort level with technical and legal issues of 401(k) plans. If you are not prepared, use a 401(k) vendor expert. Position the 401(k) vendor expert as the plan technician. Explain to the 401(k) plan sponsor that your expertise is in investing and plan participant education. You cannot afford to stumble in a sales presentation on any reasonable technical or legal question. You will compete against financial sales professionals who have a great degree of knowledge of 401(k) plans, and they may be considered the ultimate competitor in your territory. You can become the ultimate competitor. See the Resource Section for additional sources of information on 401(k) plans.

A successful 401(k) is a win for all of the partners involved.

The 401(k) market is commoditized

401(k) vendor programs look more alike than dissimilar. Many 401(k) plan decision-makers are individuals who have matured as investors and believe they can use non-traditional sources to accomplish investment goals. 401(k) vendors that do not provide for a financial sales professional to sell and service their program are chosen by plan sponsors who do not believe that you can add value to the company 401(k) plan. The plan sponsor who chooses this type of 401(k) vendor does not believe the financial sales professional can help them accomplish their corporate goals for creating and maintaining the company 401(k) plan. Many plan sponsors do not realize the benefit of working with a financial sales professional who specializes in helping individuals accomplish investment goals.

Right or wrong, some plan sponsors may transfer their individual beliefs to plan participants. Plan sponsors may possess the knowledge and confidence to work alone, but plan participants may not have the same level of investment knowledge and confidence. 401(k) vendors that sell directly without the intervention of a financial sales professional have gathered market share as a result of this perception by plan sponsors.

401(k) Sales Champion™

What about the plan participants? For many plan participants, a 401(k) program marks the first time they have invested money outside of a bank checking or savings account. Many plan participants are first-time investors, often guided in their investment management decisions by past performance or what their neighbor is doing, rather than what is best for them to accomplish their individual financial goals. They are "rear-view mirror" investors.

To break the commoditization of the 401(k) marketplace, financial service companies and non-financial service companies must focus on plan participants by supporting 401(k) Sales Champions™ to gain market share.

Don't sell a 401(k) program. Consult with the plan sponsor and recommend the best 401(k) program to accomplish their goals. Then service the 401(k) plan so the plan participants can best accomplish their individual retirement saving goals.

If you want to be known as value-added in the commoditized 401(k) marketplace, offer value-added service and pay attention to the plan participants. Success as a 401(k) Sales Champion™ will depend on whether the plan participants and plan sponsors recognize the importance of the value-added service you provide in the form of employee retirement education. Reading this book will help you understand how to prospect, acquire and retain 401(k) plans –focusing on the plan participants. Set yourself apart from the herd of financial sales professionals by helping plan participants confidently accumulate and manage their retirement wealth.

Relationships are the greatest influence on acquiring and retaining 401(k) business. If you do not have an existing relationship with prospective 401(k) plan decision-makers, you must have a well-developed business plan, persistency and the ability to demonstrate your competency to service the plan and its participants. After showing your knowledge and genuine interest in helping, you will develop a relationship with the 401(k) plan decision-makers, enhancing the likelihood of getting an invitation to make a proposal for their company 401(k) plan. The relationships you continue to build with the plan sponsor, centers of influence and plan participants through ongoing service will help you to retain 401(k) plans, and lead to referrals.

The anatomy of a 401(k) Plan

A 401(k) plan consists of five working parts that interact with each other and determine the success or failure of a plan. These parts are the plan document, plan administration, plan investments, trust services, and employee retirement education.

Plan Document
This is a legal binding contract. It contains the regulations that the 401(k) plan will abide by. It defines who the players are and what rules they must follow. The plan document explains how employees become eligible to participate, how much they can contribute, how often they can change their contribution rate, and if vesting schedules will be used for employer contributions.

PROSPECTING 4 IDEA

Vesting and eligibility requirements can help an employer to "shine-up" their company plan and make it more competitive without substantially increasing their out-of-pocket expenses. Having a shorter period of time to become eligible and fully vested can be attractive features for employees in a competitive hiring environment.

The plan document clarifies who will be responsible for making investment decisions for the plan's assets and how participants can access their money before retirement. The plan document will also state how plan participants money will be dispersed due to their retirement, leaving the company or plan termination.

401(k) Sales Champion™

It is important that employers work with plan document professionals who can help to incorporate provisions into the plan document, which can assist them in accomplishing corporate goals. Plan document design professionals are ERISA attorneys or are employed by a 401(k) vendor or a local Third Party Administrator (TPA).

Plan Administration

Essentially, a plan administrator is the bookkeeper for the 401(k) plan. The plan administrator is defined as a representative of, or the plan sponsor company in the plan document. However, many plan administration responsibilities are typically sub-contracted to a third party; a 401(k) vendor. Plan administrators are responsible for the accounting of the plan assets. Among their duties is the verification of an employee's enrollment eligibility. If the employee is enrolled, plan administrators verify with the employer that the correct amount is withheld from the employee's paycheck. Also, they make sure the employee and the employer's contributions are allocated to the correct investment choices.

MARKETPLACE **8** FACT

Current regulations impose deadlines for depositing employee 401(k) contributions. The regulations require that the employer transmit the contributions to the trust on the earliest date that can be reasonably segregated from the employer's general assets, but in no event later than the 15th business day of the month in which the contributions were withheld or received by the employer. There are significant penalties for employers who do not deposit employee contributions in accordance with current regulations. The employer would be engaged in a prohibitive transaction if timely deposits are not made. The reportable conditions that could exist are as follows:

- The transaction is considered a loan between the plan and the plan sponsor (employee)
- The DOL considers that the employer used plan funds for its benefit
- Embezzlement

continues to next page

Preparation: Enhancing Your 401(k) Knowledge

continues from previous page

According to the DOL, since October 1995, more than 1200 investigations have resulted in findings of prohibitive transactions with monetary sanctions imposed.

Source: Capital District Business Review (Albany)
"Potential risk exists in retirement plan compliance,"
June 19, 2000

When the money is invested, plan administrators are responsible for verifying accuracy of gains, losses, dividends, and interest reinvestment. They also report the plan to the employer, the plan participants and to the Internal Revenue Service and Department of Labor. Plan administrators ensure compliance with all of the rules and regulations contained in the plan document. Competent plan administration is a necessity for a well-run 401(k) plan.

Plan Investments

Plan investments are where plan participant withholdings and employer contributions are invested. Usually the employer selects and monitors the investment choices and more often than not chooses mutual funds for the plan assets to be invested. Typically, a 401(k) program permits plan participants to determine how their plan assets are invested among an investment menu of mutual funds. This mode of investment management is called **Participant Direction**. If the plan sponsor makes the investment decisions, this mode of investment management is called **Trustee Direction**. A growing trend is for plan participants to open a brokerage account and purchase any investment allowed by tax laws or the trustees. This investment management mode is called **Self Direction**.

401(k) Sales Champion™

There can be combinations of these investment management modes within a 401(k) in a tiered format. Plan sponsors can build a base program of mutual funds where participants allocate their account balance, and a second tier allowing for a self-directed brokerage account option for participants who want to purchase individual securities.

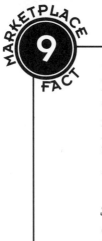

"...on a macro level, 401(k) plans run by investment firms have the most aggressive or highest allocation to equity at 68.8%. In comparison, this drops to 61.7% for plans run by insurance companies, and 55.9% at banks. While not surprising, it does mean that plan sponsors need to take this bias into account when deciding what type of firm to choose to run their plan."

Source: Institute of Management and Administration (IOMA), May 2000, "How Much Does Participant Allocation Reflect the Provider's Agenda?"

Regardless of the investment management mode the employer decides upon, they have a fiduciary responsibility to make certain the investments are appropriate and suitable for the plan participants.

ERISA (Employee Retirement Security Act of 1974) requires employers to follow certain rules in managing 401(k) plans. Employers are held to a high standard of care and diligence and must discharge their duties solely in the interest of plan participants and their beneficiaries. Among other things, this means that employers must:

- Establish a prudent process for selecting investment alternatives and service providers

- Ensure that fees paid to service providers and other expenses of the plan are reasonable in light of the level and quality of services provided

- Select investment alternatives that are prudent and adequately diversified

- Monitor investment alternatives and service providers once selected to see that they continue to be appropriate choices

Source: U.S. Department of Labor, Pension and Welfare Benefits Administration (PWBA), "A Look At 401(k) Plan Fees...for Employees, ERISA requirements of employers."

Trust Services

The Trustee of a plan is usually an officer(s) or committee formed with employees of the company. Often trustee operational duties are sub-contracted to a third party, which many times is the 401(k) vendor. Operationally a trustee is responsible for receipt, disbursement, allocation, and custody of plan assets. They have been referred to as the "cash flow" cops. When money is contributed they are responsible for ensuring that the money is invested correctly. When a distribution takes place, they are responsible for ensuring that the right dollar amount is given to the correct person.

401(k) Sales Champion™

SERVICE IDEA 5

Trustees also have fiduciary responsibilities, which are defined in ERISA. Helping the Trustees to understand what their fiduciary responsibilities are and how they can manage those responsibilities is a great way to provide value-added services to the plan sponsor.

MARKETPLACE FACT 11

The Pension and Welfare Benefits Administration (PWBA) of the Department of Labor is responsible for administering and enforcing the fiduciary, reporting and disclosure provisions of Title I of the Employee Retirement Income Security Act of 1974 (ERISA). The provisions of Title I of ERISA, which are administered by the Labor Department, were enacted to address public concern that funds of private pension plans were being mismanaged and abused. The goal of Title I of ERISA is to protect the interests of participants and their beneficiaries in employee benefit plans. Among other things, ERISA requires that sponsors of private employee benefit plans provide participants and beneficiaries with adequate information regarding their plans. Also, those individuals who manage plans (and other fiduciaries) must meet certain standards of conduct, derived from common law of trusts and made applicable (with certain modifications) to all fiduciaries. The law also contains detailed provisions for reporting to the government and disclosure to participants. Furthermore, there are civil enforcement provisions aimed at assuring that plan funds are protected and the participants who qualify receive their benefits.

Source: U.S. Department of Labor, PWBA History and ERISA

Employee Retirement Education

Even if you have a well-written plan document, attractive investment choices, efficient operations, and easy access to plan information, you could still have a plan that performs poorly. **If plan participants do not fully understand the program –and the benefit of participation –then the strength of the plan features does not matter.**

Educating employees about the value of retirement planning is critical for the success of a 401(k) plan. Plan participants must confidently know they can afford to build a comfortable retirement savings, and they should understand how to use various plan provisions and investments to accomplish their retirement savings goals.

Successful campaigns to educate employees about retirement are a result of professional use of hard copy and computer software to reinforce a positive personal presentation. Employee retirement education events should be held every six to twelve months and more often if requested by the plan sponsor. The events should be conducted by a financial sales professional and/or vendor representatives who cares about the plan participants' ability to learn and fully absorb what they hear. Whether you discuss the future value of money or recent gains or loses in the stock market, messages should be clear and concise. It is beneficial if visuals are used to help the participants digest the information. Remember much of what we learn as adults is reinforced through visual support materials.

You are not expected to be an expert in any of the five disciplines, yet 401(k) Sales Champions™ acquire a generalist understanding of all. There are professionals within your firm and/or the 401(k) vendor organization whose expertise is available to you and your 401(k) clients. **Employers and employees want to hear you say you want to become an expert in them.** They want you to help them accomplish their respective goals with the company 401(k) plan.

As the financial sales professional, you should not provide counsel for the writing of plan documents or be responsible for the accounting of a 401(k) plan. You may help the trustees choose and monitor plan investments, but you should not manage the money.

401(k) Sales Champion™

Your role is two-fold: serving as the local relationship manager for the plan sponsor and being the employees' Retirement Coach™. You are responsible for creating and maintaining a relationship with the plan sponsor and the plan participants. Operational and marketing professionals at the 401(k) program vendor should not manage your responsibilities and you should not manage theirs. You, along with professionals within your firm and/or from the 401(k) program vendor, form a team that benefits the plan sponsor and the plan participants. **Become an expert about the plan sponsor and the plan participants and you will become a 401(k) Sales Champion™.**

Should you develop a technical understanding of 401(k) plans?

Yes, you should. By developing a technical understanding, you can demonstrate a depth of comprehension to the plan sponsor and plan participant that is unmatched by your competitors. A well-rounded understanding of the tax laws, which govern qualified plans in general and 401(k) plans specifically, will allow you to deliver consultative qualities that the plan sponsors and participants desire.

Spend time with industry professionals such as ERISA attorneys, third party administrators and wholesalers from 401(k) program vendors. Join 401(k) organizations. Support your dedication to the 401(k) market by mentioning your memberships in proposals and marketing pieces. Also see the Resource Section of this book for a listing of books, associations and websites containing information on learning more about 401(k) plans.

Preparation: Developing a 401(k) Sales Champion Practice.

How do you build a 401(k) practice?

To start, grow and maintain a thriving 401(k) business, you need a plan, patience and persistence. Typically it takes three to nine months from your first cold call to a plan decision-maker(s) to land a plan. Many financial sales professionals have started and stopped prospecting for 401(k) plans because they simply had unrealistic expectations for the timeframe required in procuring a 401(k) plan, and they had no business plan (a disappointing circumstance that could have easily been avoided had there been a well-developed and executed business plan).

We hope that you will enhance or embark on your career in the 401(k) industry by developing a business plan fueled by the information in this book. Any business plan requires time to develop. Talk to financial sales professionals who have demonstrated success in acquiring and servicing 401(k) plans. Read everything possible on the 401(k) marketplace. Discuss the possibilities within the marketplace with your manager or partners. You will want their buy-in; after all, they will be impacted by the sales cycle. After you have written your business plan, start prospecting. Do not let your lack of knowledge or experience stand in your way. If you land an appointment, consider taking a 401(k) vendor wholesaler, your own firms' 401(k) marketing professional, a senior financial sales professional or manager from your office with you.

What resources are available to help you accomplish your professional goals for servicing the 401(k) marketplace?

There are many resources to help you forge a path to financial reward in the 401(k) marketplace. Lead sources and contact manager programs are among the tools we recommend. Your own firm may have valuable marketing materials and marketing professionals who can offer assistance. Do not forget that 401(k) vendors' staff professionals are available to help you. Local retirement plan professionals such as ERISA attorneys and third party administrators can also be sources of valuable insight and support.

Why do employers (plan sponsors) adopt 401(k) plans?

A strong case could be made that most employers are motivated by profit. After all, a healthy bottomline is what keeps a company afloat. Employers understand that the marketplace will dictate whether the goods or services they provide will become and remain profitable. Employers also know that the morale and productivity of their employees can significantly influence profits. In today's economy, unemployment is historically low. Employers are scrambling to find quality employees and struggling to retain them.

Tight labor markets often dictate the need by the employer to offer an attractive benefit package to employees. The unemployment rate among the civilian labor force in the 1990s has ranged from 7.8% in June of 1992 to 4.0% in June 2000.

Source: U.S. Department of Labor Statistics

Employers adopt and maintain 401(k) programs in order to attract, retain, reward and motivate quality, productive employees. Remember the days when salary alone was the key factor for employees when they sought a better job opportunity? In recent years, salary and health insurance were most important. Prospective employees are now interested in a complete package: salary, health insurance and a retirement plan. **Though many workers do not know the ins and outs of a 401(k) program, they know the value of one.** Employers are recognizing that a 401(k) plan is a valuable recruiting tool, so they are installing and continually enhancing their company 401(k) plan.

Employers also adopt 401(k) plans because of a cost perspective. A 401(k) plan can be the only type of retirement plan that many employers can afford. We have heard that approximately 10% of an employee's wages must be set aside during his entire career in order to fund an adequate level of retirement income. Many employers cannot afford to solely contribute such an amount for each employee. A large portion of the 10% needs to come from the employee. Without a 401(k) plan, an employee who earns $70,000 may be limited to a $2,000 (2.85%) IRA contribution instead of a maximum $10,500 (15%) allowed to salary defer in a 401(k) for 2000.

HR 11102 would increase the maximum limit on annual contribution to a 401(k) account to $15,000 from $10,500 in 2000. The limit would then rise with the inflation rate.

What does a plan sponsor expect from you, the financial sales professional?

Many plan sponsors have shared with us the issues they considered when reviewing 401(k) vendor programs and the financial sales professionals to service their company's 401(k) plan. In all cases their main focus evolved around these three criteria:

401(k) Sales Champion™

A They want the financial sales professional to demonstrate a sincere interest in the company and to provide the program that is best suited for their employees.

B They want assurance that their employees will not pay too much for what they receive. They wanted the financial sales professional to have a vested interest in working for them. They do not want the financial sales professional to work solely for gaining the "biggest commission." They want to work with financial sales professionals they can trust to recommend the best program for their employees regardless of the commission potential.

C Plan sponsors want to be able to rely on the financial sales professional to tell them when it is time to upgrade.

It is important to communicate and demonstrate your value-added services to plan sponsors. If you cannot convince a plan sponsor that you and your program are the best fit for his company, he will likely look in another direction, leaving you without a win. As we have stressed, most 401(k) vendor programs are similar, and competition is fierce. By demonstrating the array of services you are willing to offer, you are only solidifying your chances of earning the plan sponsor's business.

We lost a sales opportunity because, after a severe market downturn, none of the funds represented in our recommended program generated a positive return for the year. The competitor, who won the plan, showed a 401(k) program, which boasted funds with a slight year-to-date positive return after the market calamity.

In this instance, we failed to effectively communicate our value to the plan sponsor. We gave the plan sponsor reason to determine the worth of our recommended 401(k) program based on a commodity issue, such as investment performance. The plan sponsor based his decision, without any understanding of our added value, solely on short-term investment performance. We should have said to the plan sponsor,

"A fund with an investment return of 100% with no one invested in it means nothing. The awareness your employees need to benefit from an investment like that is derived through the ongoing educational support we provide."

You develop and communicate your value-added services to plan sponsors by continually enhancing your understanding and expertise in the features and benefits provided by 401(k) vendors you can represent, as well as competitors' 401(k) program offerings. As your experience with 401(k) sales grows so will your product and service expertise. Annually create or update a Vendor Comparison Fees spreadsheet for analyzing your available 401(k) program offerings and those of your competitors. Share this spreadsheet (see next page, for an example) information with your clients and prospects.

401(k) Vendor Fee Comparison

Service Vendor:	Vendor:	Vendor:	Vendor:
One-Time Fees:			
Plan Document Design			
IRS Submission Kit			
IRS Users Fee			
Recordkeeping			
Conversion Fees			
Employee Communications			
Annual Fees:			
Plan Document Maintenance			
Plan Asset Custodial Fee			
Plan Administration Base Fee			
Per Participant Fee			
Per Eligible Participant Fee			
Per Eligible Non-Participant Fee			
Discrimination Testing			
Participant Statements			
5500 Preparation			
1099 Preparation			
Loan Maintenance			
Distributions			
Section 125 Services			
Additional Fees (Y/N)			
Mutual Funds:			
Up-front Sales Charge (%)			
Back-end Sales Charge (%)			
Surrender Charge (maximum %)			
Corporate Trust Services:			
Annual Base Fee (minimum)			
Asset Based Charge			
Loan Fee			
Distribution Fee			
Employee Communication Services:			
Materials Charge			
Per Hour Charge			
Travel Expenses			
Total Fees:			
First Year			
Ongoing			

Preparation: Developing a 401(k) Sales Champion™ Practice

Communicate your value-added service to employees via retirement education events and offerings. Retirement education meetings positively impact the employees' understanding of the company 401(k) plan. At the same time, retirement education meetings help the plan prosper. **When employees walk out of an education meeting with more confidence, employers are assured that employees clearly understand the benefit of working for the company.**

A 401(k) Sales Champion™ will use employee information tools, provided by the 401(k) vendor, to help them communicate their value-added services to the plan sponsor and participants. From the plan sponsor, they acquire current plan asset allocation models, participation rates and average deferral percentages. By comparing these numbers with updated figures compiled after the enrollment process, they make these numbers meaningful for the plan sponsors. Annually, employees can be surveyed (see exhibit #2 in the appendix) about their perceptions of the company 401(k) plan. This information will then be used in an annual review for comparing previous results and for re-establishing ongoing goals. This is an effective way to quantify your value-added services to plan sponsors.

Develop service strategies for the plan sponsor to help them better monitor and document their fiduciary "due diligence" activities. Construct a three-ring binder with tabbed sections for the written investment policy, investment menu comparative matrix, employee communication goals, and employee education event materials (see page 149 for a discussion of the Plan Sponsor Book.). Keeping track of investment management and employee retirement education materials is an easy way for you to demonstrate your value-added services to the plan sponsor and enhance the retention of the plan and the relationships with the plan sponsor and the plan participants.

In the early years of 401(k), a plan sponsor went to a bank or insurance company to get the company 401(k) plan. Now, employers can go to banks, insurance companies, brokerage firms, mutual fund companies, consulting firms, third party administrators, and payroll processors for 401(k) programs. It is difficult for plan sponsors to tell one 401(k) vendor from another.

Make yourself stand out by recommending the best possible 401(k) program you can and communicating that you care about the plan sponsor and their employees. Take an active part in relationships with plan sponsors. **Do not let your firm, or 401(k) vendor, take charge of the relationship with your plan sponsor client. You take charge.** Offer to arrange conference calls and site visits with the 401(k) vendor operations professionals and the 401(k) plan sponsor. Be an advisor and make recommendations, set meetings to discuss transition issues and lead the discussions. Show them your level of commitment with the value-added services you provide. Use your energy, knowledge and abilities to empower the plan participants and help them realize that investing in a 401(k) plan is worthwhile.

A particular 401(k) plan we won reinforced our core belief of providing service to the plan participant to achieve success in the 401(k) marketplace. In this particular situation, the plan sponsor hired a consultant to aid in the search for the company's new 401(k) program vendor. The consultant narrowed the search to two finalists, a large national bank and us. What we found was that there were more similarities among both programs' features than differences.

In the final stage of the selection process, the plan sponsor allowed the plan participants to ultimately choose the 401(k) vendor. After each finalist detailed to the firm's employees what they would do for them, the employees voted.

The number of votes each employee had was determined by their account balance. For example, if John Q. Employee had $4,500 in his account, he had 4,500 votes. When the votes were counted, we overwhelmingly won the popular vote. We were chosen because we were able to communicate to the employees what we would do for them; we assured them that we would become their Retirement Coach™. **As their Retirement Coach™, we would listen to them, answer their questions and interpret information for them.** We promised and subsequently delivered.

This victory reinforced the importance of value-added service in a commoditized marketplace. Both of us presented a daily valuation program using multiple mutual fund families for the investment menu. Both programs offered a similar volume of information flow for the plan participant and the plan sponsor. We were chosen because of the unparalleled introductory and ongoing employee retirement education we promised to deliver.

How do you reinforce to plan sponsors and plan participants that you are the financial sales professional they should choose?

Plan sponsors like reassurance that you have a well-developed plan to service them and the plan participants. Simply put, they want to know the plan participants will understand how to best use the 401(k) plan and therefore, better realize the benefit of working at the company. As a financial sales professional, you must have a game plan to execute. It is essential that you recognize the importance of providing the maximum benefit and relief to the plan sponsor. Create and maintain a program which clearly informs plan participants and allows the plan sponsor to better manage their fiduciary responsibilities.

You must consistently find ways to reassure your plan sponsor clients that the services you provide are unique. The wealth of investment information is increasing every day. **Your role, as a financial sales professional, is to absorb data from the markets, process the information and offer your wisdom to the plan sponsor and plan participant clients.**

At a time when the stock market was substantially down, we called all of our 401(k) plan sponsors and offered to speak with the plan participants as soon as possible. Each plan sponsor politely declined our invitation, but every one appreciated that we showed an interest and initiative that their previous provider never demonstrated.

401(k) Sales Champion™

Like any employee benefit program, employers add 401(k) plans to attract, retain, reward, and motivate quality, productive employees. Especially in a tight labor market, where quality workers are difficult to find, employers have come to recognize the importance of offering employees more than competitive wages. Employers establish exceptional employee benefit programs like 401(k) plans and your job is to bring it to life. This makes you a valuable partner.

Describe yourself as someone who specializes in helping employers and employees fully realize the benefits of the 401(k) plan. Your role can determine the success of the program. Remember you are a partner with the plan sponsor, the plan participants and the 401(k) vendor. You help each party accomplish their goals through the 401(k) program, while accomplishing your own goals.

The ideal clients will understand the need and the value of your services. Perhaps they have never had an ambitious and motivated financial sales professional like you to promote the 401(k) program. Give the plan sponsor added reason to choose you by informing them that you help employees to confidently use the 401(k) tool to accumulate and manage the single largest pool of money that they could ever accumulate in their lives.

When you meet with plan sponsor prospects, tell them how you will increase the awareness and utilization of the company 401(k) plan by detailing how you will work with the plan participants.

PROSPECTING 5 IDEA

Tell the plan sponsor how you will help the employees to understand the three variables involved in determining how much money they accumulate for their retirement:

1 How much they save

2 How their money is invested and how well their investments perform

3 How much time they give themselves to accumulate wealth

Preparation: Developing a 401(k) Sales Champion™ Practice

The most important variable in accumulating retirement wealth is time. You want to help all employees fully utilize the company 401(k) plan as soon as they are eligible. Help the plan sponsor by delivering valuable plan support. Help them understand they would have a less successful program without you. **Build a reputation as a financial sales professional who makes a difference in helping employers and their employees accomplish their respective goals for the 401(k) plan. Take an active part and become indispensable to them both.**

To help bolster your credibility and reputation, obtain a testimonial letter from your current plan sponsor clients. Most of them are willing to grant you this favor, especially after your tireless efforts make the 401(k) plan work for their respective company. Share compliance-approved testimonial letters with your 401(k) plan sponsor prospects.

Service to the plan participants is the key to success in acquiring and retaining 401(k) plans. If you want to have a financially rewarding and personally gratifying career in the 401(k) marketplace, it is imperative that you accept the role of Retirement Coach™. As a Retirement Coach™, you can make a difference in helping the plan participants establish and accomplish their retirement savings goals. As a financial sales professional, set yourself apart from the herds of competition by providing plan participants with the competent counsel they need to effectively manage their 401(k) account. Plan participants can become long-term clients if you offer them proper guidance. Financial service companies and 401(k) vendors need to understand the importance of servicing the plan participants, by empowering you, the 401(k) plan participants' Retirement Coach™.

A relationship is the most important factor in acquiring and retaining 401(k) business. If you have not already established a

401(k) Sales Champion™

relationship with the 401(k) plan decision-makers, do it now. Demonstrating competency to service the plan and its participants is essential. After winning the plan, you will develop relationships with future prospect decision-makers through your ongoing actions with your clients.

As mentioned earlier, because of technology, the 401(k) business will become more commoditized since every financial-related firm in the 401(k) marketplace will have access to and offer similar programs. Plan sponsors will want to know what makes you different from other financial sales professionals. Expertise and service will be the key to gaining a competitive edge. Thorough and consistent education of plan participants will make the difference.

If you want to write that ticket to success, be different. Be committed to the plan sponsor and the plan participants. Show them that you are concerned about their company and their retirement savings needs.

How do you build your reputation as an expert?

To build a reputation as a 401(k) expert, begin by learning everything you can about 401(k) plans. Attend seminars and workshops. Join your local pension councils or a related group. Become an officer of the group and attend meetings faithfully. Talk to established experts. Listen to them and question them. Absorb information like a sponge.

You don't have to hold an MBA or a Ph.D. to qualify as an expert in your field. When you feel comfortable with your knowledge of the 401(k) industry, produce a compliance-approved marketing piece that explains how you operate your practice. Publish an article in the local newspaper or business journal on a 401(k) plan topic. People believe what they read, and when they see your name in print, they will identify you as an expert. Develop contacts with broadcast media outlets in your area. These relationships may lead to "face time" on television, radio or the Internet when a story related to 401(k) plans is breaking.

Perhaps the most basic tool for demonstrating your expertise in the 401(k) industry is in everyday conversation. When you are asked what you do for a living, do not tell the person you work for a certain company. Instead answer, "I specialize in managing 401(k) plans for corporations of all sizes. I help people to accumulate and manage retirement wealth through their company 401(k) plan."

Also, be sure that other professionals know what you specialize in. You can accomplish this through networking and the marketing piece previously mentioned. Send the compliance-approved literature to every accountant, third party administrator (TPA) and attorney you know.

Team selling and services – Bringing expertise together to win.

To achieve prosperity and success in servicing the 401(k) marketplace, you must service as many plan participants as possible throughout their personal financial life cycles. The number of participants and volume of overall plans you have will determine the necessity for multiple support personnel to service your plan participants. A structured team can provide focused value-added service and enhances the cross-selling opportunities. Each team member can provide insight, which can offer guidance to plan sponsors and plan participants, resulting in more efficient service.

The majority of 401(k) Sales Champions™ did not start out with a team, they evolved into a team. As your positive reputation spreads, you will likely generate more business from referrals than active prospecting. Over time, you will need to manage the growth of your practice. As your plan volume increases, you cannot afford to let service decline. You will reach a point where you cannot maintain your high service standards alone. When this happens, it is time to add to your team. After all, dedicated service to plan sponsors and the plan participants is what helped you reach the level of success you have attained.

It seems that often we hear from financial sales professionals who, working alone, lose plans to a financial sales professional with a team. For many 401(k) plan decision-makers, dealing with a team is more appealing. These decision-makers perceive that a team will dedicate the desired time and attention to their employees. Since a team has multiple financial sales professionals, some plan sponsor prospects consider them more valuable.

How do you build your team?

Members of your team should have abilities that complement your own personality style and range of product knowledge. Consider a group approach to handle each client. One 401(k) Sales Champion™ we know has a team, which consists of five financial sales professionals. Team members specialize as a 401(k) and business owner expert, a high-net-worth individual consultant, a financial planner, and a prospector/enroller.

Another team has a due diligence officer responsible for profiling the needs of the 401(k) plan sponsor prospect and working with other team members to select the appropriate 401(k) vendor(s). They also have an enrollment officer who is responsible for assessing the needs of the 401(k) plan sponsor and the employees and coordinating the fulfillment and delivery of initial and ongoing employee retirement education events. A team member is also assigned the role of relationship officer responsible for the overall satisfaction of the 401(k) plan sponsor. Successful teams have defined roles for team members and the respective team members are held accountable for executing their roles.

You know what makes your business tick. Before searching for members to fill your team, be clear about the talents you desire in a person and the roles you are trying to fill —whether it be administrative, prospecting, servicing, closing, etc. Look for potential team members who demonstrate an attitude that shows they thrive on the team concept.

Preparation: Developing a 401(k) Sales Champion™ Practice

In your practice, you will want people who are eager to do their part to attract and retain clients for the practice.

College interns can be vital team members for your practice while providing them valuable experience. Make sure that you check with your office manager or compliance officer before you have any unregistered team member interacting with the public.

Should you represent several 401(k) vendor programs?

If possible, represent multiple 401(k) vendor programs, and recommend the optimal one to the plan sponsor. You can increase the likelihood of acquiring and retaining relationships with plan sponsors and plan participants by not hinging your success on a single 401(k) vendor.

If you do not base your success on one 401(k) vendor, you diversify, just like owning several stocks, not just one. You can recommend a more appropriate 401(k) program if the current vendor causes concerns about losing the client relationship, as the result of mismanagement of your client's 401(k) program.

Your success as a 401(k) Sales Champion™ should be determined by your ability to service the plan sponsor and the plan participants.

401(k) Sales Champion™

A powerful statement to tell a prospect is that it is your responsibility to inform him when you believe his firm should use a different 401(k) vendor.

If you have access to multiple 401(k) vendors you have the ability to recommend an upgraded program as the plan matures. **A 401(k) plan gains more power and access to the market of 401(k) vendor programs based upon the plan's assets.** As the plan assets grow so does the competition among 401(k) vendors in the features and fees of their program. This is a strong rationale for you to be vigilant to assure that your 401(k) plan sponsor client has the best program working for their company.

What are the benefits for you to be consultative and recommend the best 401(k) program you can?

Within the 401(k) marketplace, there is tremendous challenge among 401(k) vendors to continually improve and outperform the competition. Representing multiple 401(k) vendors and recommending the best 401(k) program can help you be more competitive. Remember that plan sponsors are tasked with an important responsibility to choose the best plan for their employees. These plan sponsors want to feel comfortable knowing you are showing them the option that best meets their employees' needs. Your help is needed in the search process for the best 401(k) vendor as well as selecting and monitoring investments and educating participants, initially and ongoing.

If you communicate to plan sponsors that you are responsible for recommending the "best" 401(k) vendor, and if you consistently inform the plan sponsors about changes in the marketplace, you are providing a valuable service. Objectivity is a tool you can use to gain the plan sponsor's trust, and this will help you stand out in the 401(k) marketplace. **If you represent the "best" 401(k) vendors, your rivals will find it difficult to compete against you.** After all, you may be representing the same 401(k) vendors they are, but they do not communicate or deliver the same value-added service, local relationship management and employee retirement education.

The 401(k) marketplace is rapidly changing. 401(k) vendors come and go and features of their programs change. The ability to recommend a new 401(k) vendor if a client's current vendor exits the market or negatively changes their program is an important quality in retaining the relationship. One of your most prominent responsibilities is informing them of changes in the marketplace. If you are able to represent multiple 401(k) program vendors, make sure the plan sponsor client realizes this.

Compare and contrast 401(k) vendor programs. Consult with the plan sponsor and recommend the best 401(k) vendor to accomplish their goals. Then, service the plan so the employees can best accomplish their individual retirement saving goals. As a financial sales professional, cultivating a reputation for dedicated service will reap benefits for you, the plan sponsor and the plan participants. Your success as a 401(k) Sales Champion™ is dependent upon it.

When the time comes to recommend a change, be careful. You do not want to open the door for a full-blown 401(k) search. This needs to be a controlled process. Communicate to the plan sponsors that you have evaluated several alternatives and show them the best. Be sure to clearly communicate why the change is necessary, how it will benefit the company and the plan participants.

The conversion to a new plan is never easy. There will be a black-out period and other inconveniences. The end result must be worth the disruptions for all involved. However, when the new vendor is live and the assets have moved, keep in mind you may get paid all over again on 100% of the assets.

401(k) Sales Champion™

What are the expenses for an employer to establish and maintain a 401(k) plan?

Creating and maintaining a 401(k) plan is not inexpensive, and you usually get what you pay for. The benefits of a well-constructed and managed 401(k) plan far outweigh the costs.

Out-of-pocket expenses an employer will incur when establishing and maintaining a 401(k) plan include expenses for establishing the plan document, plan administration and perhaps trust services and employee communications. Some 401(k) vendors will charge for an enrollers' time and travel for conducting employee education events. Employer contributions to plan participant accounts are an out-of-pocket expense. Employer contributions are usually discretionary to a 401(k) plan, meaning the plan sponsor is not mandated to make the match and/or profit-sharing contributions.

MARKETPLACE FACT 14

Company Match Contributions

"The study found that the majority of DC plans –approximately 76% –have some type of company match. A majority of plans match at a rate of between .26¢ and .50¢ on the dollar, while about 25% offer a match higher than .75¢ on the dollar. About 20% of these participants benefit from a higher rate than 75 cents."

Source: Institute of Management and Administration (IOMA), June 2000, How Many Investment Choices Should Your 401(k) Plan Have?

The Cost of Plan Sponsorship: Average Annual Total Plan Expense (by number of participants, 1999)

	Recordkeeping, Administration	Investment Fee	Trustee	Total Plan Expenses
100 participants	$4,126	$47,005	$826	$51,957
1,000 participants	$20,140	$448,850	$2,390	$471,380
5,000 participants	$94,350	$2,203,750	$3,450	$2,301,550

Source: HR Investment Consultants; survey of 5,000 participants plans for 1999/IOMA, July 2000

Investment management costs are not normally out-of-pocket expenses, and they will become the single largest expense for the plan as it matures.

The prototype plan document is usually provided with little or no expense by the 401(k) vendor with a "bundled" program. If a custom-designed plan document is needed, an ERISA attorney will charge for their services.

Plan administration expense covers the cost of accounting for contributions, distributions as well as compliance testing. All reporting to the plan sponsor, the plan participants and the IRS are normally paid for through plan administration expense.

Plan sponsors can potentially recapture some of the dollars they spend on plan expenses with the use of vesting schedules. If an employee leaves prior to becoming fully vested, those non-vested monies can be used to offset plan administration or future employer contribution expense.

401(k) Sales Champion™

"Plan participants in 1999 picked up 38% of record-keeping fees compared to 21% in 1991. 57% of plan sponsors tell participants that they (the participants) are paying recordkeeping fees if the employer is asked."

Source: Hewitt Associates Trends & Experience in 401(k) Plans, 1999/IOMA, July 2000.

A growing number of plans are shifting total expenses –not including employer contributions –to plan participants. This trend enhances the need for the plan sponsor to be fully aware of all expenses that he is asking plan participants to bear. The plan sponsor has a legal obligation to find the best deal for the employees. Plan participants do not negotiate with program vendors, the plan sponsor does. Offer your services to the decision-makers to compare the costs of the competing vendors.

SALES IDEA

2

Complete the Department of Labor Fee Comparison Worksheet and suggest that other competitors complete the form as well. You will find a DoL Fee Comparison Worksheet, Exhibit #4, in the Appendix of this book. Decision-makers may be hesitant in sharing your competitors' information with you. You need to communicate to them that you do not mind if they share your recommendation with competitors.

SALES IDEA

3

You may want to consider securing an agreement with the plan sponsor whereby you will be responsible for comparing the various 401(k) vendors, and your fee for acting as a search consultant will be offset from any compensation paid to you by the chosen 401(k) vendor.

"For further information regarding the level of fees typically charged to 401(k) plans and 401(k) plan fees and expenses generally, see the Pension and Welfare Benefits Administration's Study of 401(k) Plan Fees and Expenses, available on the PWBA's web site at: http://www.dol.gov/dol/pwba."

Source: U.S. Department of Labor Pension and Welfare Benefits Administration, PWBA A Look at 401(k) Plan Fees...for Employees.

If you are competitive and up-front with cost, you will be the victor in this strategic leg of the sales "battle."

What are the costs of establishing a 401(k) plan?

Investment management and opportunity lost are the greatest costs in a 401(k) plan. **Investment management fees will be the greatest known cost to a 401(k) plan. Opportunity lost will be the greatest unknown cost to the 401(k) plan.**

The majority of assets in existing 401(k) plans are managed with mutual funds. Mutual funds can charge external and internal fees to those plan participants who invest their money with them. External cost for mutual funds are the sales loads, up-front or back-end. The internal expenses are the management fees and 12-b-1charges. Many mutual funds waive up-front or back-end sales loads once a 401(k) plan accrues over $1 million in plan assets, or when trustees sign a Letter of Intent specifying when (i.e. 13 months) the plan will have over $1 million invested with the fund family. So sales loads will disappear over time. Internal management fees of mutual funds are why investment management fees will become the largest "known" expense for a

401(k) Sales Champion™

401(k) plan. Mutual fund management fees and 12-b-1 charges are assessed on the total dollars invested within the fund. As an example, if a 401(k) plan has average management and 12-b-1 fees of 1.5 percent, and the plan has $1 million in assets, then the fee to manage the plan assets is $15,000 a year. As the plan assets increase to $2 million, the investment management expenses will rise to $30,000. The fee is deducted from the gross performance of the investment choices.

MARKETPLACE FACT 18

The Report's most important finding is that mutual fund fees have declined.

- 85% of large equity funds reduced their fees during the nine years studied by the GAO.
- The average fee reduction identified by the GAO was 20%.
- The GAO found that fund fees generally reflect economies of scale that result in lower fees.
- 89% of funds that experience significant asset growth during the 1990s reduced their fees.
- The GAO's findings are consistent with academic and ICI research on this subject.

The GAO report studied data from the 77 largest mutual funds between 1990 and 1998. The GAO urged that mutual funds should be required to give individual investors information detailing exactly how much they paid in operating expenses.

Source: Investment Company Institute (ICI), Summary of the Investment Company Institute's Response to the General Accounting Office (GAO) Report on Mutual Fund Fees, July 5, 2000.

The greatest "unknown" cost to a 401(k) plan can be the opportunity lost levied against both the employer and employees in plans with less than optimal participation. **If less than optimal participation is ongoing then the employer will not have complete assurance that their goals for creating and maintaining the plan can be realized.**

Preparation: Developing a 401(k) Sales Champion™ Practice

In addition, earning potential for all participants can be affected by less than optimal participation. **Without complete and full participation by lesser-compensated employees, some highly compensated employees may not be able to save the maximum dollar amount allowed under tax laws.**

Eligible employees who do not fully utilize the 401(k) plan will find themselves, one day in retirement, wishing they had. **The time will arrive when every one of us will not desire to or be able to generate income from our labors. We call that moment in time the beginning of our retirement years. For every moment thereafter, the quality of our life can be determined by how well we saved while we were working.**

MARKETPLACE FACT 19

The Social Security Administration will send you a personal earnings and benefits estimate statement that shows the benefits you and your family are eligible for if you retire, become disabled or die. To order call 1-800-772-1213 or visit: www.ssa.gov.

Source: CBS MarketWatch.com, "Retirement resources, free information flows from U.S. agencies," Marshall Loeb, July 31, 2000

What are trustees' fiduciary responsibilities?

Fiduciary responsibilities are real and you should seek information from local ERISA Attorneys as well as resources listed in the Resource Section of this book to develop a good understanding of ERISA and fiduciary responsibilities. You will be a more effective marketer of 401(k) plans if you do. Helping the 401(k) plan trustee(s) manage their fiduciary responsibilities is a great way to provide a valuable service.

401(k) Sales Champion™

"...A finance executive handling pension investments is held to a higher legal standard of performance than one handling corporate investments. With the latter, the executive is held to the prudent-person standard. Under ERISA, however, this defense has no weight, because, in regard to pension investments, one must demonstrate the prudence of an expert. If a fiduciary is sued in an ERISA case and loses, the full extent of his or her wealth is at risk, whereas with corporate investments, an executive has no personal liability. Indeed, it was the government's intent in drafting ERISA to utilize personal liability as the law's teeth."

Source: CFO Magazine, CFO Buyer's Guide: 401(k) Providers, April 2000, "Defending Your 401(k)," Russ Barnham.

According to the 401(k) Answer Book, "A fiduciary is a person who exercises any discretionary authority or control over the management of the plan or its assets, or who is paid to give investment advice regarding plan assets. The definition depends on the functions a person performs and not on the person's titles. Plan service providers such as actuaries, attorneys, accountants, brokers, and record-keepers are not fiduciaries unless they exercise discretion or are responsible for the management of the plan or its assets."

With the perceived "gaps" in Regulation 404(c) understanding and enforcement, along with unsophisticated and or unsuccessful plan participants, you have a recipe for an understandably nervous 401(k) plan trustee(s) when it comes to the proper management of their fiduciary responsibilities.

MARKETPLACE FACT 21

Three federal government agencies have authority to investigate possible violations of the rules for private pension plans and to bring lawsuits or assess penalties against individuals engaged in illegal actions; the Department of Labor, the Internal Revenue Service and the Justice Department.

Source: U.S. Department of Labor Pension and Welfare Benefits Administration, PWBA.

MARKETPLACE FACT 22

Complying with 404(c) is an "all or none" proposition. This means that a plan must comply with ALL articles of 404(c) to access the fiduciary protection desired. What to look for:

Here are the main items you should be looking for:
• Does the plan allow participants to choose from a broad range of investment alternatives that meet certain criteria? At a minimum, your plan should have at least three different investment choices with material-different risk and return characteristics.

• Does the plan allow participants the opportunity to exercise control over assets in their accounts, and are they educated on a routine basis to ensure they know how to exercise control over their accounts. Further:

a. Participants must be permitted to make transfers among investment alternatives with a frequency commensurate with the volatility of the investments, but not less than quarterly.

b. Participants must be able to give their investment instructions to an identified plan fiduciary who is obligated to comply with those instructions. (Registered Investment Advisor, Trustee, Administrator, etc.)

Continued on next page

401(k) Sales Champion™

Continued from previous page

- Making sure the participants understand what they are trying to accomplish, and how their chosen funds are going to help attain their goals is critical. Allowing participants to wander aimlessly, even if you have periodic educational meetings, is dangerous. You may not know who "gets it" and who does not, so a good follow-up system should be implemented. It is important to proactively communicate, ask the right questions and responses on it until the participants understand. This ensures that your employees have interpreted and internalized the educational and investment data into something that is useful and meaningful. Problems occur when expectations and reality don't match.

- Complying with 404(c) should not be a casual thing. It is intended to require rigorous and diligent fiduciary efforts to ensure participants are being taken care of.

Source: 401(k)HelpCenter.com, July 31, 2000, "Sued By Your Own Employee?", Matthew D. Hutcheson, President, MDH Consulting, Inc. Originally published in the newsletter of the Oregon Legal Management Association.

Not one, but two ways to construct a 401(k) plan?

There are two ways to build a 401(k) program; bundled and unbundled. A bundled 401(k) program has only one vendor for all five disciplines. With an unbundled 401(k) program at least two vendors share the servicing of the five disciplines. For example, a brokerage firm may handle the plan investments, employee education tasks, and trust services, while a TPA firm provides the plan document and plan administration services.

Bundled or unbundled? –
How to know which 401(k) program is best for your plan sponsor

The answer to this question depends on many factors, all of which revolve around features the plan sponsor wants for the company 401(k) plan, and the expense they are willing to agree to.

As the answer to the previous question explained, with a bundled arrangement one vendor provides all five disciplines for the 401(k) plan. In some cases, one vendor will have the program under its label, but the vendor will have subcontracted one or more disciplines (such as administration) to an outside firm. Bundled programs can offer greater efficiencies with contributions, reporting, distributions, and access to information because they can employ more technology. If a plan sponsor says they prefer one contact for all operations of the 401(k) plan, tell them about a bundled program. **Bundled programs can be less expensive than unbundled programs because the 401(k) vendor could be receiving revenue from the mutual funds used as investment options, which can help offset plan administration expenses.**

An unbundled program has multiple vendors to supply work for each discipline. Typically with an unbundled program, one vendor supplies plan document and plan administration services, and a second vendor supplies investment management and employee education functions. An unbundled 401(k) program can employ either a daily valued or balance forward recordkeeping system.

Unbundled 401(k) program buyers prefer the flexibility to leave an individual vendor if they are not providing optimal service. The unbundled 401(k) program allows clients to correct a specific problem without disrupting the entire plan. Unbundled programs also provide the plan sponsor more flexibility with plan document design strategies. Those design strategies can aid certain employees with the amount of employer contributions they receive (i.e. new comparability plan documents).

First-time plan sponsors are comfortable with local specialists. They have learned to rely on local experts to help their business, (i.e. CPA, attorney, personnel firm). First-time plan sponsors who employ less than 100 employees may be more apt to implement an unbundled program. Why? Because the employer can learn from specialists. Local vendors are geographically close, which allows plan sponsors to meet with clients, walk them through reports, and teach them how to manage the plan. This arrangement is helpful because plan sponsors benefit from having an environment that nurtures their confidence and matures their experience with managing the company 401(k) plan.

Of course, as the financial sales professional in an unbundled program, you are like a parent of multiple children. When something is broken, you may be forced to deal with finger-pointing.

SALES IDEA 4

For your benefit, align yourself with local TPAs who are highly regarded for delivering exceptional administration services in your region. First-time buyers are concerned about cost. Second-time buyers are more interested in competent service.

A TPA we know says that bundled program providers are in business to sell investments. All other plan disciplines, he believes, are considered overhead. **Vendors of unbundled programs are dependent upon the successful completion of their discipline for their respective profitability.**

Understand how to sell and construct both bundled and unbundled programs. After profiling the plan sponsor you will be better able to recommend the appropriate 401(k) plan construction.

Daily valuation vs. balance forward record keeping – Which is better for your plan sponsor?

The easiest way to answer this question is to understand the employer's goals for the 401(k) plan. If a primary objective is providing employees with easy access to their account information, daily valuation record keeping is the answer.

We have seen balanced forward record keeping used predominately in new plans where there is a quarterly or less frequent valuation. Balanced forward record keeping is also typically used when a trustee directs plan investments and the employer does not think it is important for plan participants to access information about assets they do not manage.

Many existing 401(k) plans started with a balance forward record keeping system (with an annual, semi-annual or quarterly valuation) before shifting to a daily valuation system when the plan sponsor believed his employees would appreciate and properly use it. There are fiduciary and staffing concerns that the employer will weigh when deciding which record-keeping system, balance forward or daily valuation to institute for the 401(k) plan. Some employers may not want their employees to have access to their money 24 hours a day, seven days a week. Perhaps the temptation is to great to change investments too frequently, damaging the long-term nature of the 401(k) plan, and lessening the impact of dollar cost averaging and asset allocation. Of course, these employers also know there could be a risk of not allowing employees to redirect their funds when markets are volatile.

There are lots of opinions when the subject of daily valuation and balance forward record-keeping arises. Keep yourself open to all of them. The plan sponsor can present the future change from balance forward to daily valuation as an enhancement to the plan participants. Plan sponsors will want to provide to the plan participants enhancements to the plan on an ongoing basis. Remember that you are a consultant to the plan sponsor. Your mission is to make recommendations that will best meet the plan sponsor's needs.

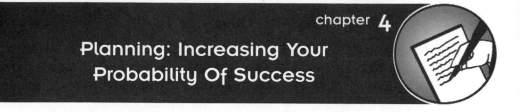
A business plan is essential

Have you ever heard the saying, "Any road will get you to where you want to go as long as you don't know where you are going"? Thus it is essential, if you want to take the "fast track" to becoming a 401(k) Sales Champion™, you have to have a business plan. A business plan can help you to use your time efficiently as well as remind you of your potential success when you feel like giving up. Take your initial energy and enthusiasm for pursuing 401(k) plans and for one-week channel it into the development of a business plan. **You have the potential for great success, so take yourself seriously and put your goals, objectives and processes in writing.**

Business Plan Writing Assistance Web sites:
www.bizproweb.com, www.bplans.com,
www.bizplans.com, www.edgeonline.com,
www.entreworld.org.

There is an abundance of individual prospects as compared to institutional 401(k) plans. You can prospect and service individual clients with multiple products to help them build their wealth, enhance their tax situation and coordinate college or estate planning among other items. With a smaller pool of potential customers, a defined business plan is essential to acquire 401(k) plans. The lead-time to acquire a 401(k) plan is greater, as well as the distance between successes compared to prospecting for individual clients. It typically takes three to nine months between the prospecting and client acquisition stages. To achieve financial reward, you must have your pipeline full of prospects while servicing new 401(k) clients. To build a successful 401(k) business, you must manage your time efficiently prospecting for clients while meeting the needs of existing plan sponsors, and individual clients.

When creating your initial 401(k) business plan, focus your attention on Level One activities, which include writing a mission statement, documenting goals and establishing the structure of your 401(k) practice.

Level One Activity – Creating Your Mission Statement

A mission statement communicates to you, your team members, your prospects and clients a clear vision of what you see your services accomplishing for all parties involved with your 401(k) practice.

> **Sample Mission Statement:**
> The ABC Team will provide 401(k) services that will allow plan sponsors to implement a competitive 401(k) program.
>
> The program will allow employers to meet their corporate goals of attracting, retaining, rewarding, and motivating quality employees.
>
> We will educate all plan participants and empower them to accumulate and manage the single largest pool of wealth of their lifetime.

Refer to the mission statement when meeting with prospects during prospecting and sales presentations. Use your mission statement to inform plan sponsors what your value-added services include, why you are unique compared to your competitors and why they should choose you to service their company 401(k) plan.

Most companies you visit will have a mission statement on the wall of their front lobby. **If you do not know what you stand for, how will the plan sponsor know?**

Level One Activity –
Documenting Your Goals

To become a 401(k) Sales Champion™ you must know what it is you want to achieve. Milestones are achieved when goals are set and put into action. Establish three sets of goals; acquisition activity, sales and service for retention.

Acquisition activity goals are created by listing:
- Number of contacts that will be made per day
- Number of qualified prospects to be identified daily, weekly, monthly, etc.
- Number of discovery meetings scheduled or attended with defined timeframe
- Number of proposals written during a defined time period
- Number of sales presentations quarterly
- Completion of specific marketing initiatives

To acquire 10 plans in 5 years...

☑ Each week I will qualify 2 prospects. By the end of the year I will have a total of 100 qualified prospects.

☑ Each quarter I will generate 2 proposals. Over 5 years I will generate at least 40 proposals from the 100 prospects I have qualified.

☑ Each quarter I will go on 1 initial sales presentation. Over 5 years I will have made 20 initial sales presentations.

☑ I will close 50% of the plans I make presentations to. Over 5 years I will acquire 10 plans.

Sales goals include: (see page 12 for an example)
- The number of acquired assets
- The dollar amount of first-year commissions
- The dollar amount of commissions and trailers in subsequent years
- The number of employers and employees turned into individual clients per year
- The number of referrals from employers and employees a year

Service for retention goals include:
- Planning and implementation of employee education events
- Completion of employer service events

Set realistic goals and develop appropriate activities to accomplish your goals. **Manage and monitor your progress, and make any necessary adjustments to accomplish your goals. Remember to reward yourself when you accomplish a goal.** Whether it is an afternoon off, a night on the town or the purchase of something extravagant, a reward serves as a reminder to you why 401(k) business is worth the work.

Level One Activity –
Establish 401(k) Practice Structure

Initially, you may be the sole practitioner; a jack of all trades. As your success grows, so should your team. Team members will help you manage prospecting, selling and servicing events. You may evolve into the role of team director, delegating specific responsibilities to respective team members. As time passes, and your practice burgeons, the roles of your team members will become more specialized.

Team members should have other specialties that complement your own. If you get the 401(k) "bug," you may not want to deal with individual accounts. A partner that flourishes on individual relationships may be the perfect fit for the cross-selling opportunities your 401(k) plans present.

A senior broker, someone with an established book of relationships in your community, may also be a great fit. Many of a senior broker's clients are decision-makers for their own company's 401(k) plan. Thus, taking a senior broker as a partner provides you with a great referral source.

Another possible team member could be someone who specializes in the administrative side of the business. A 401(k) plan can have operational service issues arise from time to time, necessitating someone who can patiently bring the plan sponsor client and the 401(k) vendor operational personnel together to solve those issues.

Why should you partner for 401(k) plans?

Partnering is done to acquire and service a specific 401(k) plan, not necessarily to form a long-term team. By partnering for 401(k) plans with another financial sales professional, you can acquire plans which otherwise might have been politically unavailable. If you do not have strong relationships with decision-makers at a company with a 401(k) plan, but you do have time and energy, partner with another financial sales professional in your office who has the contacts but lacks the enthusiasm to pursue and service 401(k) plans. Perhaps partner with the "corner office" professionals in your office. Other great partners are "office rookies". Quite often they have the enthusiasm to find many 401(k) prospects, but lack the skills to close the sale. Splitting commissions and assets appropriately is a win for both of you. It's important to note that partnering can also demonstrate a depth of local support which may be unmatched by your competitors.

Of course, partnerships are as susceptible to squabbles between partners as with any other union. Implementing effective communications among members certainly will lessen any tensions. Use a partnership contract, which succinctly defines roles and responsibilities of each partner. The contract should also discuss commission sharing, cross-selling opportunities and ongoing service responsibilities. Commissions are allocated to the partners in a variety of ways. A 50%/50% split is standard, yet it may be wise to motivate partners to accomplish specific roles. For instance, one partner could simply be rewarded for ongoing contributions and cross-selling opportunities, and another receive the up-front and a share of trailer commissions to act as the local relationship manager with the plan decision-makers. The first is motivated to provide initial and ongoing service, with the latter rewarded for uncovering the opportunity and staying involved with the plan. Please refer to the next page for a sample Partnership Contract that you can use in establishing an account team.

RETIREMENT PLAN SERVICES
PARTNERSHIP CONTRACT

1.) All 401(K) accounts that work with the *(name of team)* will remain the property of the referring financial consultant.

2.) Any suggested course of action, client contacts, or account activities will be cleared first with the referring financial consultant prior to any contact with the client, unless the referring financial consultant suggests otherwise.

3.) The *(name of team)* will provide to the referring financial consultant all available resources to ensure the opening and retention of 401(K) accounts. These resources include, but are not limited to:

- initial coaching
- discovery meeting with the client
- formal proposal preparation
- implementation meeting with the client
- follow-up throughout the implementation process
- preparation and delivery of all employee education campaigns
- ongoing client consultation
- ongoing reviews with third party administrators

4.) For the above listed services, *(name of partner)* will enter into a production credit sharing agreement with the referring Financial Consultant. This agreement directs a 75% / 25% split of production credits, 75% to the referring Financial Consultant, 25% to *(name of team)*. This revenue sharing agreement will be in effect for one year, and can be altered by the referring financial consultant.

5.) Upon completion of the first year anniversary date, *(name of partner)* will meet with the referring financial consultant to structure an agreement for the continuation of services for the second year.

financial consultant   *(name of partner)*

_____   _____

Effective Date of Agreement:_____

Anniversary Date Renewal:_____

(This is a sample for illustration purposes only. Consult your office compliance officer or local attorney for appropriate partnership language.)

Planning: Increasing Your Probability of Success

From the initial contact with the prospect, through the sales presentations and the ongoing servicing of the client, the partnership contract must specifically detail roles and responsibilities. If the contract becomes void, there should be an amicable clause to divide the relationship among partners or place the plan with one of the partners.

Is a regional/national/ international team viable?

Constructing a network of domestic and international fellow financial sales professionals will help you to be perceived positively by multi-location and multi-national firms.

With a regional/national/international team, you will seem extremely valuable in the eyes of multi-location and multi-national firms. When dealing with these types of companies, it is imperative to deliver an identical message to all employees and site managers. With a team of dedicated financial sales professionals located throughout the nation and/or world, you are better able to deliver consistent, effective retirement education and support to the plan participants and site managers.

Level Two Activities – Bringing Your Business Plan to Life

As you identify the opportunities that you or your team would like to realize, it will be time to take your business plan to the next level with Level Two Activities, including:

Establishing Vendor Partnerships - Which 401(k) vendors will you represent? Discussion to follow in Chapter 5.

Implementing Prospecting and Profiling Activities - How will you execute the process of developing prospects into clients? You will find instruction for prospecting and profiling activities in Chapter 6 and 7.

Sales Presentation Process - How will you present solutions to your plan sponsor prospects and help them to choose you to service their company 401(k) plan? Instruction for completing a compelling sales presentation can be found in Chapter 8.

Implementation Process - How will you ensure that the recommended program is successfully launched? What activities will you be performing along each step as you begin to grow your business? You will find discussion of how to successfully implement a 401(k) program in Chapter 9.

Ongoing Service - What ongoing support will you be providing in order to become indispensable to the plan sponsor and the plan participants, to retain them as clients? Instructions and helpful tips for providing ongoing service like a 401(k) Sales Champion™ can be found in Chapter 10.

chapter 5

Planning: Establishing Vendor Partnerships -Which 401(k) Vendor(s) Will You Represent?

Who is the 401(k) vendor wholesaler?

The wholesaler for a 401(k) vendor can be a mutual fund, insurance company wholesaler or a 401(k) specialist at your or another firm. No matter how the individual is employed, the 401(k) vendor wholesaler is a member of your team when you represent their firm's 401(k) program.

You are the local relationship manager for the plan sponsor and the employee's Retirement Coach™. The 401(k) vendor wholesaler is responsible to the plan sponsor for representing the 401(k) vendor's program. The 401(k) vendor's wholesaler is also responsible for bringing the vendor's resources to aid the 401(k) plan sponsor in ensuring they are pleased with the 401(k) program once the relationship has begun.

Successful wholesalers are masterful at convincing and communicating effectively. Wholesalers of 401(k) programs can be a good source of competitive information as well as a "coach" to help you continue developing your 401(k) selling skills.

What are the qualities that employers look for in a 401(k) vendor program?

First-time 401(k) plan sponsors have a tendency to look at the cost of the program versus any other features you may present. An employer who installs a 401(k) plan for the first time typically is less sophisticated in judging the attractiveness of features and discerning the differences among 401(k) vendor programs. First-time buyers may not be aware of the qualities of vendor programs that could enhance the success of their company 401(k) plan. Many times convenience of an existing personal or business relationship and low perceived cost are the qualities that help them to choose their first 401(k) vendor(s) for their company plan. In addition, a first-time buyer may have purchased the 401(k) program from an individual with whom they have an existing personal or business relationship. Taking a 401(k) plan away from a friend of the buyer is difficult.

As the company 401(k) plan matures, plan sponsors want vendors that have demonstrated competency in delivering services necessary for the plan to be positively perceived by the employees. Plan participants and plan sponsors alike want to have a 401(k) vendor who has name recognition and a demonstrated history of providing good service.

Operations, investment management along with name recognition and staying power of the 401(k) vendor has a greater focus for the plan sponsor as the 401(k) plan matures. Plan participants want accurate information and timely reporting, as well as instant access to account information and good investments with low expenses. As a plan participant's account balance increases, typically so does their investment savvy and desire for enhanced plan features.

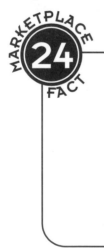

"As an automated, mass-customized experience (401(k) management), the business lends itself to technological solutions, and the (plan) participants are eager and willing to alter their habits. Providers and sponsors who recognize this reality will continue to lead the marketplace. Those that don't, will inevitably be left behind."

Source: 401kWire.com, "New Technology Works!,"
John Rekenthaler, June 15, 2000.

Which 401(k) vendors will you represent?

Existing 401(k) plans are preferred by 401(k) vendors. Not only will they make more in initial fee income, 401(k) vendors believe that experienced plan sponsors have solid expectations of the 401(k) vendor as well as what the 401(k) vendor needs to provide in order to have an effective operating 401(k) program. Plan sponsors want a 401(k) vendor who has staying power. Plan sponsors do not like to change 401(k) vendors. However, if faced with the option of putting-up with poor service from a 401(k) vendor or financial sales professional, change is inevitable.

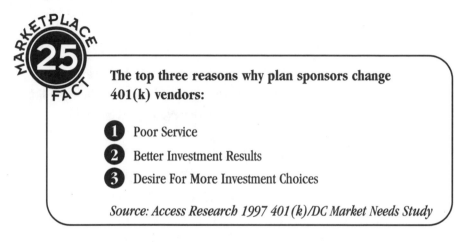

The top three reasons why plan sponsors change 401(k) vendors:

1. Poor Service
2. Better Investment Results
3. Desire For More Investment Choices

Source: Access Research 1997 401(k)/DC Market Needs Study

The plan sponsor wants an efficient use of company operational resources. Employers have out-sourced this employee benefit program. Experienced plan sponsors realize they will get what they pay for from their 401(k) vendor(s).

What should you know about the 401(k) vendor(s) program?

As you interview the 401(k) vendor(s), listen carefully when they tell you about their company's commitment to the 401(k) marketplace and the competitiveness of their program.

Commitment

Capital - Is the 401(k) program vendor spending enough money to maintain a strong overall program, including operational personnel, technology of the record keeping systems, marketing materials, and quality wholesalers?

Quality Professionals - Are the wholesalers the types of individuals who can help you grow in the business? Can they help you acquire plans and provide counsel to assist you with better servicing the plan and the plan participants?

Sales Support - Will senior management of the 401(k) vendor get involved with the sale? Will your prospect be able to tour their facility with their appointed operational day-to-day contact? What is the client service relationship manager ratio to plans?

Assigned and Consistent Operational Contact Person - Is the turnover of operational personnel excessive? Will clients encounter a revolving door of operational contacts? Turnover among 401(k) vendor staff members can lead to trouble for your client. Verify tenure of the vendor's staff members and ask the wholesaler tough questions like, "Why are operational professionals attracted to your company?"

Staying Power - There will be consolidation among 401(k) vendors in the years to come. Will your client purchase services from the acquirer or the vendor being acquired?

Competitiveness

Investments: Multi-Fund Family Capabilities - Perhaps you and the employer believe that a 401(k) program should have the capability to invest in multiple mutual fund families.

Access to Information: 1-800 Number and Internet - How can plan sponsors and plan participants access information?

Which 401(k) vendors will you represent?

Fees for Investments - What is the overall internal expense ratio for each of the recommended choices? How expensive are the investments (including management fees, mortality expenses, operating expenses, etc.)? Are there up-front and back-end sales charges or surrender penalties?

Fees for Administration - What specific reporting and testing service does the 401(k) vendor provide and what are the charges for these services?

Fee Discount Policy - Do administration fees decline as the average participant account balance grows?

Guarantees: Service to Plan Sponsor and Plan Participants - Does the 401(k) vendor stand behind their program by guaranteeing service delivery? What will the 401(k) vendor do if service standards are not met or if the plan sponsor or you are displeased?

Operations - Is the 401(k) vendor investing in technology to create greater efficiency and customer service? Is there Internet access by participant phone center personnel to answer plan participants on-line?

Presentations - Are presentations from the 401(k) vendor(s) effective? Can the 401(k) vendor print proposals for a union 401(k) plan through a union shop and have the union bug inserted?

If you are bidding for a union 401(k) plan, and you are not personally delivering the proposal, make sure that the proposal is couriered by a union-represented organization like the United States Postal Service.

Financial Sales Professional Support - Will they respond quickly to your requests? Will they supply "tools" like financial planning and asset allocation programs that you can use to enhance cross-selling and incubation qualities of the relationship? Can the plan participant cue the interactive voice response system (IVR) or web site so they can be connected directly to you to converse about investment management and personal finance issues?

As you become more successful in the 401(k) marketplace, you should expect a higher level of support from 401(k) vendors. They should offer training for you and your team, workshops for your prospects and clients. They should also conduct presentations to educate and retain your 401(k) and individual clients.

Once you have interviewed prospective 401(k) vendors, make a spreadsheet of all of their program features. This spreadsheet can become a powerful tool in supporting your dedication and consultative approach to a 401(k) plan sponsor prospect.

How do you decide which 401(k) vendor programs to represent?

You should choose to represent 401(k) programs from those vendors who realize the value-added support that you can provide to the plan sponsor and the plan participants. Some 401(k) vendors do not hold the financial sales professional in the same regard as they do the plan sponsor or plan participants. Many 401(k) vendors believe their respective program sells itself. Their client is the plan sponsor, not the financial sales professional. Too many 401(k) vendors do not realize the benefit of recognizing the financial sales professional as a critical partner in retaining the plan sponsor relationship and the plan participants' assets for their firm.

Understand the unique qualities and strengths of particular 401(k) vendor programs. All vendors offer unique qualities. When you understand these qualities, you can make the best recommendation to 401(k) plan sponsors. Discover what sets apart the respective 401(k) vendor from their competitors.

Some examples of unique qualities can include tenured talent of their operational team, self-directed brokerage account availability, a multiple mutual fund family investment platform, service guarantees, technology such as a "paper-less" operational environment, Internet access or perhaps professional enrollers who specialize in adult education instruction. **Ask the 401(k) vendor wholesaler what unique qualities of his company's 401(k) program he stresses in a sales presentation.**

You will want to know if the 401(k) vendor is going to support you from prospecting to implementing, as well as provide you ongoing support to insure retention of the 401(k) plan relationship. Before recommending a particular 401(k) vendor, ask their wholesaler to provide you with the names of two financial sales professionals out of your territory who currently use their program. Interview the individuals and ask them questions pertaining to the service provided by the 401(k) vendor. Be sure to include the following questions when interviewing the referrals. Their perspective will be invaluable to you.

 Is the 401(k) vendor client relationship manager handling your client's plan qualified, responsive and tenured?

 Is your client satisfied with the service they receive from the 401(k) vendor?

3 Does the 401(k) vendor make your life easy?

4 Is your compensation accurate and paid on a timely basis?

When you acquire the 401(k) plan, your focus will be on servicing the plan participants and the plan sponsor, not maintaining administrative issues. If the 401(k) vendor does not manage their responsibilities, they will inhibit your desire and ability to grow your business.

How can the 401(k) vendor wholesaler help you to acquire and retain 401(k) plans?

A 401(k) vendor wholesaler should be your trusted partner. They can help you develop your business, conduct discovery meetings, prepare proposals, complete follow-up calls, and provide leads.

Some financial sales professionals are reluctant to involve 401(k) vendor wholesalers because they are concerned that the wholesalers will discuss their prospects with other financial sales professionals. Honesty and integrity are vital traits to look for in your 401(k) vendor wholesaler.

401(k) vendors seek to hire wholesalers who demonstrate tenacious sales skills. Others are hired for their knowledge of selling retirement plans. Both types of 401(k) vendor wholesalers can help you succeed.

401(k) vendor organizations can provide you with many tools and benefits. Leads, "door prizes" and speakers for workshops are among the benefits 401(k) wholesalers and their respective employers may offer.

The 401(k) vendor wholesaler's selling skills are critical to your success in marketing the 401(k) vendor's program to your prospect. The 401(k) vendor may have an outstanding program, but if its wholesaler does not properly represent the program, there may not be a sale. **When the 401(k) vendor wholesaler has selling skills that complement your own, it can increase the probability of success when you market to a committee, which may consist of multiple decision-makers with different personality traits.**

The wholesaler represents the 401(k) vendor organization and they are rewarded if the plan sponsor chooses their company's 401(k) program. The wholesaler should be relied upon as the expert in his company's 401(k) program and should do everything possible to promote his company's program. The 401(k) vendor wholesaler should effectively communicate to you and the plan sponsor how his company's 401(k) program can best help the plan sponsor accomplish his corporate goals

Which 401(k) vendors will you represent?

for creating and maintaining the company 401(k) plan. **If you do not use the 401(k) vendor wholesaler in the sales presentation, you can face a disadvantage to your competitors because he likely can speak about his company's program more effectively than you can.**

You must be able to carry the sales meeting. You should create an agenda and run the meeting. Even if you have not mastered the technical expertise of 401(k)'s, a well-run meeting is always impressive. The agenda you create should be based on the plan sponsor's goals. The 401(k) vendor wholesaler should simply detail his company's program qualities and answer questions. You are responsible for showing the 401(k) plan sponsor that you are dedicated to delivering value-added services via local relationship management and employee retirement education. You must demonstrate experience and gain confidence from the 401(k) plan sponsor in your ability to provide quality service to them and the plan participants. You must also communicate accountability. Plan sponsors may be uncomfortable with the administration being done in a far away city. They need to know that you are the first line of defense and accountable for their total satisfaction with the 401(k) vendor program.

Do not depend upon the 401(k) vendor wholesaler to close your sale. If you rely upon the wholesaler for the close, you are not capable of communicating your value to the 401(k) plan sponsor. **You may be able to only present the second best program to a 401(k) plan sponsor, but if you communicate greater value than the sales person showing the best program, you can win.**

All viable 401(k) vendors will continue to develop their programs so one will have a feature lead over the others. Commoditization will continue to be a central theme among 401(k) vendors. You will be the difference. **Your value-added services bring the 401(k) vendor's program to life. You are the unique quality in an otherwise common environment.**

What is the key to 401(k) prospecting success?

The secret of success is the consistency of purpose. **Persistence is the key to success in prospecting 401(k) plans.** So many outstanding financial sales professionals have started and stopped prospecting for 401(k) plans because they did not have a realistic understanding about what was involved in acquiring 401(k) plans. Most commission-earning transactions that you undertake can be completed within days, if not hours. With 401(k) plans, the time from initial cold call to close could be three to nine months. You need to formulate achievable activity and sales goals in order to enhance your ability to win 401(k) business.

What is the prospecting process?

Include in your business plan the following 10 steps involved with the prospecting process:

1 Analyze your current book of business for contacts and leads.

2 Acquire additional leads and verify mailing information.

3 Load verified lead information into a contact manager database.

4 Begin the direct mail/e-mail campaign.

5 Follow-up with decision-makers, complete the initial questionnaire. Record information into the contact manager.

401(k) Sales Champion™

6 Set a date and time for the discovery meeting.

7 Conduct the discovery meeting and complete the discovery meeting questionnaire.

8 Compile discovery meeting notes for the lead and post into the contact manager database for use in preparing proposals.

9 Move the prospect to a "warmer" database.

10 Conduct sales presentations and fulfill follow-up issues.

Lead database providers: www.dnb.com, www.freeerisa.com, www.judydiamond.com, www.larkspurdata.com, www.mmdaccess.com, www.mobiusg.com, www.pensionplanet.com

The leads you have should consist of companies you want to work with. The first action after acquiring leads is calling the company to verify mailing information. If you purchase leads, the data on the lead could be six to 18 months old. Names, addresses and other information may have changed. If you are about to embark upon a direct mail/e-mail campaign, you want to send information to the correct person, with their correct title, to their correct address.

Understand where in the company the 401(k) plan decisions are made. Is it with the CFO, or is it with human resources or perhaps a committee consisting of the above mentioned professionals plus employee representatives?

Prospecting for 401(k) plans is not solely an exercise to acquire clients. It should also be a means to promote your practice and enhance your team's reputation in the community. Prospecting in the form of direct mail and e-mail includes introductory letters and letters that inform prospects of changing 401(k) marketplace conditions and alerts prospects of forums, which your team will sponsor.

Following are a few sample letters that you may use in their entirety or simply for inspiration. Make sure your compliance officer reviews all prospecting materials before the public reviews them. Direct mail and e-mail prospecting efforts, and word-of-mouth praise from plan sponsors will enhance your team's reputation in your community. Direct mail and e-mail prospecting letters should incorporate compliance-approved testimonial letters from clients, which attest to your quality service. As the competitive environment for 401(k) plans heightens, your reputation will play an increasing role in the plan sponsor's decision to choose you over your competition.

Dear XXXXXXXX,

"All 401(k) service providers are the same. They signed up my plan and then left us cold. The ongoing support isn't what they said it was going to be!" We hear that a lot from 401(k) plan sponsors. You may have said it yourself.

Our 401(k) plan sponsor clients, on the other hand, enjoy the broadest retirement plan services enabling them to establish and maintain an effective retirement program for their employees. Harnessing the resources of our own local, focused creativity we strive to provide unparalleled support for our 401(k) plan sponsor clients. Our clients understand that we continually seek to exceed their expectations.

We start with your employees – providing a program that gives them the knowledge and confidence to take advantage of their employer-sponsored plan. We believe that focusing on your employees will help you accomplish your corporate goals for establishing and maintaining your 401(k) program.

I will be calling you soon to begin a dialogue and to ultimately earn the privilege of competing to provide services for your company's 401(k) plan. Thank you in advance for the opportunity.

Sincerely,

Your Name Here

Dear XXXXXXXX,

As a sponsoring employer of a 401(k) program you understand that there are major objectives to accomplish in order to determine whether your 401(k) plan is successful or not. Those objectives include, an above-average employee participation rate and deferral percentage. We have found that there are three reasons why 401(k) plans suffer from low participation rates and deferral percentages:

#1. The employees do not understand why they should participate.
#2. The employees do not believe that they can afford to save for retirement.
#3. The employees do not understand or trust the investment choices.

Our responsibility to our plan sponsor clients is to ensure that each eligible employee completely and confidently understands the potential benefits of participation in the 401(k) savings plan, through initial and ongoing retirement education. Our retirement education program is conveyed through in-person presentations, supported by printed and electronic materials. The paramount objective of our retirement education program is to ensure that you as the plan sponsor receive credit for maintaining the 401(k) savings program, thereby enhancing the employees' benefit of employment with you.

We would like to have the opportunity of discussing further how we can help your employees realize the terrific benefit you have provided for them. I will call soon to arrange a convenient time to discuss how we can help your employees realize the benefit of their participation in your organization's 401(k) savings plan.

Sincerely,

Your Name Here

Dear XXXXXXX,

Many of my corporate clients have asked me to help them improve their company's 401(k) plan.

With a generation of baby boomers approaching retirement age amid concerns about the future of Social Security, company sponsored retirement plans, especially 401(k) plans, have become more important to the companies that sponsor them and their employees.

A well-designed 401(k) retirement plan enables employees to save for their retirement through pre-tax salary deferrals and provides important benefits for your company. Combined with your overall benefits package, a 401(k) plan is an excellent tool for attracting and retaining quality employees.

I believe the (name of the 401(k) vendor program) is the right 401(k) plan for the needs of your company today and the future. This program offers you:

1) A mutual fund family covering the full spectrum of investment styles.
2) A number of other fund families to choose from representing over (a number) of total funds as well as a brokerage account option.
3) A state-of-the-art daily valuation recordkeeping and administration service.
4) Customized employee retirement education events to maximize employee participation and goodwill.

I will call you soon to arrange a convenient time to discuss your company's 401(k) plan in-depth.

Sincerely,

Your Name Here

Where should you look for prospects?

The best place to look for 401(k) prospects is your current book of business. Who do you know that owns a business, is a decision-maker at a business, is an employee or who knows an owner, decision-maker or employee at a company with a 401(k) plan? Many times, your individual clients will not be satisfied and will refer you to the company 401(k) plan decision-maker. Talk to clients who are decision-makers for their respective firm's 401(k) plan.

Some 401(k) Sales Champions™ prospect high-net-worth individuals, of which some are business owners or decision-makers at companies with 401(k) plans. With this approach, they acquire their individual business first, build rapport, and then seek their company 401(k) plan.

Leverage into existing relationships. If you have current plans within a particular zip code or personal relationships with decision-makers at companies within specific zip codes, this is an ideal starting point. Ask current clients, who are participants in their own company's 401(k) plan, about the quality of employee retirement education or investments. Ask for the name and number of the human resources director, CFO, president or other potential decision-maker. Call that person and offer to conduct a free, no obligation, investment education workshop for their employees or review of the current investment choices. Be prepared to show the 401(k) plan decision-maker samples of what you can provide.

Search the Internet, read the local newspaper, review business guides and chamber of commerce directories for companies you want to pursue. Interview the centers of influence in your area (CPAs, attorneys, etc.). Tell them your specialty and stress the value-added service you provide. Remember to thank any person who refers business to you. Golf balls, a calendar or a dinner may bring you your next multi-million dollar 401(k) plan referral.

If you take the time and think, you can find prospects just about anywhere. You will find them at the theater, in the ballpark and on the golf course. Drive around industrial parks and write down addresses and names of companies. Do not be afraid to strike up a conversation and tell the person you are talking to that you specialize in 401(k) plans. It is possible that person is a decision-maker for a prospective company.

Perhaps the conversation will lead to more business for your practice. Networking is an extremely effective tool to locate prospects. When you introduce yourself to decision-makers as a 401(k) plan specialist, they will tell you everything you need to know. Likely, they will say who is currently servicing their company 401(k) plan. They will be sure to detail any problems they are experiencing. If you know your market and your competition, you will probably know the problems your prospect is encountering before he tells you. Remember, open your mind and realize any business is a potential client. **When they become your clients, each payday at the company is your payday, too.**

Be focused with your prospecting. Remember to get 10-20 plans you may need 100-200 leads. **Finding plans is simple; landing them is the challenge.**

What are some non-traditional prospecting ideas?

Conduct workshops for plan sponsors where they can hear independent experts provide valuable information. Past workshops we have participated in include the following topics:

- "How To Conduct A Search for A New 401(k) Vendor"

- "Are You Paying Too Much For the Company 401(k) Plan?"

- "How To Better Manage Your Fiduciary Responsibilities"

- "Should You Have More Than One Mutual Fund Family In Your Company 401(k) Plan?"

- "Enhancements In the 401(k) Marketplace Among 401(k) Vendors"

These workshops can be done in-person or via a conference call.

Conduct a golf outing inviting plan sponsors, CPAs and an ERISA attorney, and have the ERISA attorney talk about fiduciary management. Obtain continuing education credits for those CPAs attending.

Survey local companies and employees about their opinions concerning their company plan and the entire 401(k) marketplace. Provide the results to your 401(k) plan prospects and local newspapers. You will not only develop a great understanding of your prospects; you will also demonstrate valuable consultative qualities and an expert opinion. (See Exhibit 1 in the Appendix for an example)

How do you build and manage a database?

Your hard work will be wasted without implementing a system to track your prospects. The contact manager you use is a great tool to remind you of upcoming events and due dates for current clients and prospects, and to help you manage those prospects who you will more actively pursue in the months and years to come. Time is money, so a refined database is essential to maximizing your effectiveness. You will want the database to be easily accessible by all team members.

After mailing an introductory letter, and conducting the subsequent follow-up phone call, separate the database so future mailings and follow-up phone calls will be directed to "warm" prospects. Consider splitting the database in two. The first could contain prospects that inform you that no change is planned for at least a year. The second database could include "warm" prospects, plans that could change within the year. Prospects in the first receive direct mail only and fewer follow-up calls. Prospects in the "warm" database receive direct mail and a follow-up call after each mailing.

Further divide each database into manageable size groups, such as 20-30 leads each. This will help you manage your daily mailing and contact schedule. To help you manage the information you will receive from the prospect throughout your many contacts, set up a cover page with the following broad categories:

- Company Information and History
- 401(k) Plan History
- Plan Specifics (rules, demographics, etc.)
- Goals/Objectives of the Employer
- Your Opinions and Comments
- Important Information to Include During the Sales Process

By segmenting information, your ongoing management of the prospect will be made easier. Wait before removing prospects from the database because they were rude or obnoxious. Give them another chance when you make a follow-up call six to eight weeks later. Remember, you may have yet to reach the 401(k) plan decision-maker.

Consolidating the prospects in your database is perhaps the most effective measure that can aid your efficiency. Countless marketing campaigns have proven that it is better to service prospects that want to be serviced rather than attempting to convert prospects that express no interest. You are not in the religion business. Having a well-developed lead database will help you to maintain a "perpetual motion" marketing program.

For a low-tech solution to a computer database, consider purchasing a dry marker board. The board should be large enough to list and keep track of your primary prospects. Divide the board into columns. Head the columns with the following information: company name, plan assets, number of participants, discovery meeting date, proposal due date, sales presentation date, and implementation date. Then keep the detailed information in the prospect 401(k) plan file.

How do you overcome objections from the "gatekeeper" receptionist as you attempt to initially verify lead information?

Receptionists can sometimes make you feel that they were hired expressively to keep you away from decision-makers of the company 401(k) plan. Though in some cases this is true, you need to get through them and accomplish your goal of discovering who in the company is responsible for making 401(k) decisions.

Here is a favorite objection you may hear when asking, "Who at the company is responsible for determining who the company 401(k) plan vendor will be?"

> **Receptionist objection:** "I cannot give out that information."

> **Your response:** "I understand. The reason why I am calling is that our team provides services to help make sure that your 401(k) plan provides maximum benefit for ALL employees. (PAUSE). Who is the chief financial officer at the company?

When is the best time of year to begin contacting prospective 401(k) plan decision-makers?

There is no bad time of the year. The 401(k) sale is a long-term process, and it will likely require multiple contacts with the 401(k) plan decision-maker before you are awarded the plan. There are examples of speedier decisions, but it will likely require multiple contacts with the 401(k) plan decision-maker before you are awarded the plan.

Most plans were created with a calendar date of January 1, so the majority of 401(k) plans change vendors on January 1 of any given year. Working backwards, in March of the previous year, your discussions with 401(k) plan sponsors should begin. The second busiest time to change 401(k) vendors is July 1, followed by April 1 and October 1 of any given year. Prospecting for 401(k) plans is a year-round process. Plan sponsors decide to create or enhance their company's plan throughout the year. More 401(k) vendors are offering incentives, like lower conversion fees, if the plan converts on a non-peak time like April 1 or October 1.

When beginning your 401(k) practice, prospecting 1 to 3 hours a day may be adequate. Determine how much time you will spend prospecting in your business plan and with your manager. Because of the long lead time, be sure your managers sign-off on this use of your time.

The best time to call plan decision-makers is early in the morning 7:30 a.m. to 9 a.m. or late in the afternoon 3:30 p.m. to 5:30 p.m. Quite often in the morning the decision-marker is answering the phone as the screener has not yet arrived at the office. Late in the day a plan deci-sion-maker may be more receptive to a long call as they are clearing their desks and preparing for the next day. We have also had great suc-cess late on Friday afternoons.

Is there a better market time – up, down or sideways – to prospect for 401(k) plans?

Service will usually be the main reason why plan sponsors change 401(k) vendors. Service delivery is not related to market activity. **Perhaps plan sponsors may be less likely to change vendors during an up or down market, but sooner or later they will grow tired of poor service.**

Although service is the key to being a 401(k) Sales Champion™ in our opinion, keep your eyes open for performance opportunity. From time to time, your competition may make an investment mistake. If you hear of or read about a competitor's funds faltering be prepared to take advantage of the opportunity and attack.

Who at the prospect company should you contact first?

Always attempt to contact a decision-maker for the company 401(k) plan. At a small company, the owner is usually the ideal contact person. A large company's decision-maker is often a Chief Financial Officer or Director of Human Resources or other executive-level manager. Larger companies typically have 401(k) committees. On your first initial contact, ask for the person responsible for determining who the company 401(k) plan vendor will be.

It is easy to be fooled about who is actually the 401(k) plan decision-maker at a company. Often a company's CFO or HR director is only collecting 401(k) program information. The company owner or president may be the true decision-maker.

It is imperative that you speak to an actual 401(k) plan decision-maker. Be persistent on this issue, as your odds of acquiring the plan increase dramatically when you tell your story to the "right" person. Don't get discouraged if you have to start with a non-decision-maker. Win them over and the gates may open to an introduction to the decision-makers.

PROSPECTING
13
IDEA

Perhaps an individual client of yours knows whom to contact at the company. Speak to those 401(k) decision-makers at companies who are current individual clients of yours. If you do not ask them about their firm's 401(k) plan and express interest in servicing it, you lose your chance of accomplishing a high probability sale.

How do you open the initial call to the 401(k) decision-maker?

Perhaps you help a client invest a distribution they received from their ex-employer. Call the employer and tell the decision-maker, "I just helped Jane Moneysaver invest her rollover distribution from the company retirement plan and I noticed that it took a long time for the check to be disbursed. Untimely disbursal is usually a sign of operational problems. There are programs, which make distributions two days after receiving all information. I service 401(k) plans and would be happy to introduce you to an enhanced 401(k) program."

This is the magic prospecting question. It works with 401(k) plans as well as all other prospecting efforts. If you enjoy sales at all, this is when the fun begins.

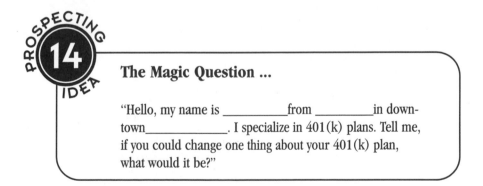

PROSPECTING **14** IDEA

The Magic Question ...

"Hello, my name is _____from _____in downtown_____. I specialize in 401(k) plans. Tell me, if you could change one thing about your 401(k) plan, what would it be?"

Don't say another word. Just wait. If the answer is anything but, "I wouldn't change a thing," you have an instant prospect.

Your next goal is to see how upset you can make your prospect. You need to drill like a dentist. Give no anethesia when inflicting your questions of pain.

Here are some responses you will want to give, when your prospect cries out in pain.

> "The statements are always late."
>> • Do your participants complain?
>> • Does that take time out of your day?
>> • Does the president of your company complain?

> "We never hear from anyone."
>> • Who is educating your employees?
>> • Don't they think your plan is important enough to service?
>> • Are you doing all their work?

> What else would you change?

While the prospect is telling you about the horrors of their current provider, you should be taking furious notes and asking more questions. Do not offer solutions or start to sell. **You will not win the plan on this call.**

Do not ask the decision-maker if he is happy with their 401(k) plan. If the answer is yes, the call is over. If he tells you just one thing he would change about the plan, take advantage of the opportunity. If he tells you his statements are always late, ask him, "How does this impact your plan." If he responds that participants often complain to him, ask him, "Do the employees have a Retirement Coach™?" If the decision-maker says he would change nothing about the current plan, ask him, "What do the employees say about the company 401(k) plan?" If he still resists, ask if he is the sole decision-maker for the company 401(k) plan and if you can remain in contact with him. He may not be in a position to talk with you right now. Asking open-ended questions allows the plan sponsor prospects to provide you with an abundance of information, which enhances the probability of acquiring them as a client.

When the prospect is done and there are no other complaints, close for the appointment.

> "It is obvious that you and your plan participants deserve more. I'll be in your area Tuesday and Thursday of next week. What day should I stop by?"

PROSPECTING IDEA 15

The goal of your initial contact with the prospect is to build rapport and to discover as much as possible about the current plan and any problems that they may be experiencing.

The purpose of the initial contact is to qualify the prospect and determine if you want to do business with them and if so, when. The next contact may be a follow-up phone call at another time or a discovery meeting. Mail a thank you letter with your card to every plan sponsor that you have an initial contact with. You can standardize this letter for efficiency and your prospect will appreciate your professionalism. Send information on you and your team, perhaps a team brochure. Be hesitant on sending any 401(k) product information to the prospect until you have the opportunity to conduct the discovery meeting. Your competitors will be eager to send product information, so be unique. **If you are asked by the 401(k) plan decision-maker to mail something on your program, inform them that you will not know what is appropriate for you until you have had the opportunity to complete the discovery meeting and close with, "I will be available Tuesday or Thursday next week at either 10:30 a.m. or 2 p.m., which is better for you?"**

How do you qualify a 401(k) plan prospect and what are the most applicable profiling questions to ask during the initial contact?

Qualify 401(k) plan prospects by asking quality questions which, when answered, provide sufficient information to determine if you want to do business with the 401(k) plan prospect. 401(k) plan decision-makers have been conditioned to brush you off the phone or out of their office quickly. Understand what you want to accomplish when qualifying a prospect. With experience, as with most things, you will acquire a more efficient sense as to whether you want to pursue the prospect company 401(k) plan. Your mission during initial contacts with the decision-makers is to determine whether you want to conduct business with a particular company 401(k) plan. Yes, be picky with which prospects you want to do business with. **Not every prospect deserves to be your client and there are many more 401(k) plans than quality financial sales professionals who want to effectively serve them.**

Here are initial profiling questions for existing plans:

1) If you could change one thing about your current 401(k) program, what would you change?
2) How long has the company 401(k) plan been in place?
3) Why did the company establish the 401(k) plan and what goals are you trying to accomplish with the 401(k) plan (attraction, retention of employees)?
4) Who decides who the company 401(k) vendor will be?
5) Who is currently providing services for the company 401(k) plan?
6) What problems with your current vendor(s) do you want to solve? Better service? Lower cost? Better investments? Better support for employees?
7) What do your employees say about the 401(k) plan?
8) When you decide it's time to upgrade, what features would you want for the new 401(k) plan?
9) Will you conduct a review of your 401(k) plan this year?
10) And finally... Are there any circumstances, like current business relationships or family ties, that will cause you to favor one vendor over another?

Profiling: Discovering What You Need To Know
In Order To Win The 401(k) Plan

Question #10 is a very important question to ask because you want to compete on a level playing field. You want to be told upfront if you don't have a chance because an in-law or friend will be awarded the plan.

Here are four quick questions you can ask if you sense the prospect is hurried:
- Who is your current vendor?
- What would you like to change about your current plan?
- When do you review the plan?
- Is it time to upgrade the company 401(k) plan?

What are some appropriate questions to ask a decision-maker who is just starting a 401(k) plan at his company?

- Who do you want the 401(k) plan to benefit most?
- What goals do you want to accomplish with the 401(k) plan?
- What have you heard about 401(k) programs from peers the media, etc.?
- What do you know about this area's providers, like banks, insurance companies and brokers?
- What features do you want for your company 401(k) plan?
  - Daily valuation?
  - Internet access?
  - Multi-mutual fund family investment opportunities?
- What is your timeframe to implement?

How do you respond to questions and objections from the 401(k) plan decision-makers?

Questions and objections are a way for a 401(k) plan decision-maker to show interest or identify areas of need. Your most important job right now is to listen. Do not overlook the objection. All objections are legitimate. Assume that 401(k) plan decision-makers raise objections as a result of past experiences or advice from trusted advisors. Confirm the objection. State that you understand, and then answer the objection with facts. When you are finished addressing the objection, ask if they have any other questions. If you are confident in your answer, reply to the 401(k) plan decision-maker, and then get back to profiling. **If you do not have full confidence in your answer to a question, tell the 401(k) plan decision-maker that you will respond within 24 hours with the answer, and do so. Decision-makers will respect you for your professionalism, then continue with your profiling.**

If you have a 401(k) plan decision-maker that says he will only deal with a trusted, current financial sales professional, your only hope lies with your persistence. Tell him you understand that you hope your clients think of you in similar ways, and ask permission to stay in contact.

Here is a common objection you will hear from a 401(k) plan decision-maker during your prospecting efforts:

Objection: "We just changed 401(k) vendors."
Answer: "That's great. What are the qualities of your new 401(k) vendor that caused you to choose them? What was the process you used to choose your new 401(k) vendor."

The answer to this question will help you understand how to compete effectively in the future. You should have very low expectations that they will be your client within two years. So ask for a referral, "What companies in the area do you know that may be reviewing their 401(k) plan?" and "Would you give me a contact name?"

What are common 401(k) start-up plan objections?

Objection: "It costs too much to start and maintain a 401(k) plan."
Answer: "If you are able to quantify the impact of retaining and attracting quality, productive employees, the 401(k) plan may prove to be a very inexpensive benefit. Recaptured employer contributions by vesting schedules can be used to offset plan expenses."

Objection: "I do not have the staff to manage the plan."
Answer: "After the initial set-up of the plan, the extent of your staff's involvement is simply to communicate to the 401(k) vendor new hires, terminations and contribution amounts. Your plan will be assigned a professional administrator by your 401(k) vendor, and they will be responsible to assist you."

Once all of your questions have been answered, you are ready to close for the discovery meeting. Closing for the discovery meeting is handled most effectively in one of two ways:

I am going to be in your area on Tuesday and Thursday at 10:30 a.m. and 2:30 p.m. (give choices), what time can I stop by and introduce myself?

or

I want to schedule an appointment to meet with you and further explain how we can help you enhance the ABC Company 401(k) plan. When would you like to meet, Tuesday or Thursday (give choices)?

What do you do when the call is going nowhere?

First, determine if you have the "best" 401(k) plan decision-maker on the phone and ask yourself, "From what I know do I want to pursue this plan?" If the call is not reaping the intended results, ask the prospect for a business referral. It is a small world. Ask. "No" will be the worst response. After all, the relationship was going nowhere to begin with.

Perhaps you challenge the prospect with this "Hail Mary" approach when the call is going nowhere: "Maybe we are not right for you. You seem satisfied. Our program(s) is (are) geared toward companies that want to provide the least expensive, feature-rich 401(k) program possible. Can you give me the names of companies who may be deciding to upgrade their company 401(k) plan?"

Be ready to react by speaking about specific features of your program(s) and setting up a discovery meeting. Remember that things change. Let the prospect know that you would like to remain in touch with them through periodic phone, mail and e-mail contacts.

What is the progression of a 401(k) plan prospect?

1) Dormant to Cold: After you have verified information on the lead and loaded it into your contact manager system.

2) Cold to Warm: After the discovery meeting has been held and the plan could change vendors within the next year.

3) Warm to Hot: At least one sales presentation has taken place and they are going to decide who their new 401(k) program vendor will be within the next 6 months.

These are suggested activities to conduct with your 401(k) plan decision-makers as they progress from dormant to hot.

Dormant to Cold: Contact the lead and verify information

Cold to Warm: Drip mail, e-mail campaign, cold walking, telephone/in-person profiling, discovery meeting, deliver "first call" marketing materials from the 401(k) vendor, deliver the team brochure

Warm to Hot: Proposals, sales presentations, follow-up letters, and materials

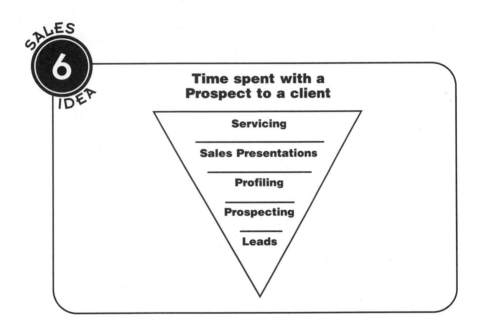

How do you manage the time between initial contact and the discovery meeting with a prospect?

We believe that you can enhance the probability of attaining the 401(k) plan by staying in contact with the 401(k) plan decision-makers as they proceed from your initial contact to the discovery meeting.

Contact the 401(k) plan decision-maker with follow-up items when you told him you would. Send an article of interest to the 401(k) plan decision-maker(s). Any way you can keep the lines of communication open with the 401(k) plan decision-maker(s) can enhance your probability of success. Use e-mail when necessary. Many decision-makers will respond on their own time as opposed to risking a lengthy phone call.

After you have acquired 401(k) plan clients, ask them for a testimonial letter about how you improved their company 401(k) plan, increased participation, generated higher savings rates and a better asset allocation model for the company 401(k) plan. Send the compliance approved testimonial letter with a prospecting letter as part of your "drip" mail, e-mail program.

Demonstrate your quality service standards during the prospecting process.

Another component, which could be part of your drip mail campaign, is a team brochure. Mail the team brochure to prospects that you have initially profiled or use as a leave-behind piece after a face-to-face meeting. The team brochure should contain biographies of team members as well as your team mission statement and description of the scope of your business.

What is the purpose of the discovery meeting with a 401(k) plan sponsor?

The purpose of the discovery meeting is to continue the process of understanding what you need to know about the company, the employees and the 401(k) plan in order to enhance the probability of being selected as the new provider. We have gone on many more sales calls than the actual number of 401(k) plans we have acquired. The number one reason why we were not chosen by every 401(k) prospect is that we did not know what we needed to know in order to be chosen. It is during the discovery meeting that you communicate your value-added service, and ask questions to completely profile the decision-maker(s) about the company 401(k) plan. More important than simply asking questions, you want quality responses. You want better answers than your competitors will receive. You can get these answers by helping the 401(k) plan decision-maker(s) understand that you are unique and you will become indispensable to the success of the company 401(k) plan. When the 401(k) plan decision-maker(s) feels that you are knowledgeable and committed to the 401(k) marketplace, you will have the advantage over any competitor.

How should you conduct the discovery meeting?

Start the meeting by telling the 401(k) plan decision-maker(s) that you would like to further explain who you are, who your team is and why you believe you are offering unparalleled services for the local 401(k) marketplace.

Explain to the 401(k) plan decision-maker(s) your mission statement and why you are doing what you do. Keep your introduction short. At the end of the discovery meeting, you will have a chance to sell. **Demonstrate your capabilities and beliefs with a brief presentation via a notebook computer or flip chart book.** We developed a pitch book, which we present during discovery meetings.

There is certain information that you should gather from the 401(k) plan decision-maker(s). The most productive discovery meetings are those where you know the questions that need to be answered but conduct an open discussion. Once you return to your office, organize your notes.

Categories of information to get from the 401(k) plan
decision-maker(s) during the discovery meeting include:

- Company history
- Company overview
- Plan history
- Problem areas (if it is an existing plan)
- Features desired
- Personal information on the decision-makers
- Valuable features other vendors have spoken about
  that interested the decision-makers
- Decision-maker names and their beliefs for the
  company 401(k) plan

SALES
7
IDEA

During the discovery meeting, have the 401(k) plan decision-maker(s) rank their concerns from most to least important. Also, have them rank features or qualities they want for their new 401(k) program. You will use this information during your sales presentation.

The discovery meeting is also the time to determine any hurdles you
must overcome to be chosen. Ask if the plan sponsor is serious about
changing 401(k) vendors. If you neglected to ask during your initial
questioning, ask if he will look more favorably upon a potential 401(k)
vendor because of an existing personal, business or family relationship.
Ask the plan sponsor what their process will be for selecting the new
401(k) vendor. Be sure to understand how the final decision will be
made and who is making that decision. There can be so many variables
involved in making a decision and you need to know all of them.
Show the 401(k) plan decision-maker that you are the ideal choice.
Bring samples of your employee retirement education materials. Be prepared to show the prospect illustrations, which reinforce your points.
If the 401(k) plan decision-maker(s) tells you that plan participants
have a difficult time understanding tax-deferred compounding, simply

show an illustration. The discovery meeting is a time when you gather information, which will increase your probability of winning.

What profiling questions do you ask during the discovery meeting?

Plan Demographics
- How many employees do you have at ABC Company?
- What is the eligibility requirement to join the ABC Company 401(k) plan?
- How many eligible employees do you have?
- How many eligible employees participate in the ABC Company 401(k) plan?
- How often during the year can eligible employees enter the plan?
- What is the average deferral percentage for the lesser-compensated employees?
- How many shifts do you have?
- How many locations do you have?

Plan Operations
- Do you process payroll internally or through an outside vendor?
- How often do you transmit payroll and contributions to your current 401(k) vendor?
- What is the company match formula?
- Do you allow the plan participants to direct all sources of contributions, including any company contributions, or only their salary deferral money?
- How often can plan participants reallocate their investments?
- How often can plan participants change their savings rate?
- How often do plan participants receive statements?
- How soon after the quarter ends do the plan participants receive their statements?
- What do your plan participants say about the statements?
- Does the ABC Company 401(k) plan allow for loans and/or

401(k) Sales Champion™

hardship withdrawals?

- Are any withdrawal provisions being abused?

Ask your prospects, during profiling, their company match formula and determine the average in your territory (perhaps distinguished by professional, manufacturing retail and service companies). Your prospects will ask you what other companies do, and this is your chance to demonstrate your expertise.

Investments

- How many investment options are there?
- What are the investment options?
- What is the disparity between the best and worst performing investment choices?
- What is the most recent value of the plan?
- Do you have a written investment policy in place?
- If there is a policy, how have the plan investments performed versus the benchmark indices?

The mean number of investment choices in 1998 was 8.4 and 47% of plans had between 6-10 choices for participants to choose from.

Source: Spectrum Group Participation Attitudes and Behavior Study, 1998

Profiling: Discovering What You Need To Know
In Order To Win The 401(k) Plan

- What types of issues arise, i.e., payroll transmission, compliance testing, etc., which you need to work through with your customer service manager at the 401(k) vendor?
- How do you feel about those experiences?
- How many customer service managers have you had in the past few years?
- What enhancements do you want to make to the company 401(k) plan and the weight you will place on those qualities (investment performance, cost, service, statement quality, and timelines, etc.)?

What should you listen for during the discovery meeting?

The phrase, "You have two ears and one mouth; listen twice as much as you speak," is a very appropriate strategy for the discovery meeting. The 401(k) plan decision-maker can also give you quality insight to their response with voice inflection and body movements.

Be focused on the 401(k) plan decision-maker and do not interrupt them as they answer your questions. Interrupting them may be perceived as being rude and may prevent them from delivering the real answer to your question. Keep your ears open for information and opinions from the 401(k) plan decision-maker that will aid you in promoting the recommended 401(k) vendor's program and your personal service. Perhaps the prospect says his employees complain about the timeliness of receiving their statements. Maybe he feels his employees are not receiving close attention. Sometimes you will have to "dig" to discover the true issues.

How can you respond to a 401(k) plan decision-maker when they state, "As a result of poor service from the current 401(k) vendor, participation in the 401(k) plan is declining"?

The key to plan participation is the implementation of a well thought-out education program. If chosen, you will be expected to provide a program for the company using enrollment sessions, posters, payroll stuffers, and most importantly, one-on-one employee meetings.

If the 401(k) plan has a company match, you should be able to guarantee 85% participation and deliver 90%. Without a company match, 70% is realistic.

Show the decision-maker tools, which they can use immediately to reinforce the plan to the plan participants. Recommend that the plan sponsor implement a long-term treatment by providing a series of payroll stuffers, and offer to conduct a "reminder" presentation to reinforce to plan participants the necessity of their participation and to re-join the 401(k) plan. By providing immediate ideas and tools, along with service to the 401(k) plan decision-maker, you will enhance the probability of being awarded the 401(k) plan.

What should you promise your 401(k) plan decision-maker prospects?

Promise your prospects only what you have control over – your value-added services, local relationship management and employee retirement education. **Under promise and over deliver.** Let the 401(k) vendor make the promises concerning their program.

What is the proposal process?

Proposals are a process. You and the 401(k) vendor(s) you present will not be selected before multiple presentations take place, especially with an existing plan. There are call-backs and the field narrows with each round. You must be prepared to offer new insights and benefits during each round.

The proposal process is a series of proposals, which gradually builds. By the final presentation, you clearly address the client's concerns gathered from the discovery meeting and all previous presentations.

The proposal process begins with the discovery meeting. You never want to be in the proposal production business, yet you may be forced to create a proposal without a discovery meeting when the prospect wants to make an imminent decision. Conducting the proposal process under these circumstances is at best a crap shoot. You should not take the time to publish a proposal until after the discovery meeting has taken place. It is critical that you and the 401(k) plan decision-maker(s) share an understanding about their goals for the plan and how your capabilities can help to accomplish them. Also, you should prioritize features the 401(k) plan decision-maker(s) wants the company plan to be driven by. Once you know the goals and priorities, it is then time to formulate and effectively share your recommendations with a written proposal.

You can quickly discern a financial sales professional who occasionally does a 401(k) versus a 401(k) Sales Champion™ by the quality of information delivered throughout the proposal process. Financial sales professionals who "dabble" in 401(k) use a 401(k) vendor's proposal as a "stand alone," one-time piece. **401(k) Sales Champions™ see proposals as an evolutionary process to assist the decision-makers in determining why they should be chosen to service the company 401(k) plan.**

Consider standardizing your written message in the form of an executive summary to be joined with the proposal that the 401(k) vendor(s) provides. Though each prospect is unique, the operations of a 401(k) program are standard. When you standardize your message, you will present the same ideas again and again, so you will become more confident with each subsequent presentation. You may present one or more 401(k) vendors to your prospect. Your standardized executive summary could include comparative matrixes to demonstrate your valuable consultative skills.

The executive summary will contain information that is unique to your team, such as an agenda and sample employee education meeting exhibits. Ask the decision-maker if he thinks this information would help him gain a clear understanding of your presentation. If it does, ask him to request that other bidders produce the same items. Set the standard in your community. Become the ultimate 401(k) competitor.

How do you work with 401(k) plan search consultants?

Plan sponsors are hiring search consultants to assist in the selection of a new 401(k) program vendor. Independent search consultants have increased in numbers. They specialize in finding 401(k) vendors for plan sponsor prospects. The search consultant could also be the company's CPA, attorney or another professional. The search consultant can actually aid in your selection, assuming that you represent an optimal program and you have cultivated a reputation for value-added services. An independent professional search consultant can make sure

Presenting Solutions: Effectively communicating
your value and solutions

that all 401(k) vendor programs are judged on a level playing field. Meet with the search consultant and explain how you service the 401(k) marketplace. Ask them how they do their job and learn from their focused efforts. You will learn that search consultants can be a rich source for prospect referrals, giving you insight about when a 401(k) plan may be available.

Search consultants usually have extensive experience with the various disciplines of a 401(k) plan. Once applicable, share your experiences and recommendation of search consultants with prospects. Offer names of search consultants to interview and potentially hire. If you are able to make these kinds of recommendations, likely prospects will see you as a financial sales professional who encourages competition. They will also appreciate your objective recommendations, strengthening your reputation as an expert advisor.

What is a Request for Proposal (RFP)?

Search consultants use request for proposals (RFPs) to gather data from 401(k) competitors for their clients' 401(k) vendor search. An RFP is a way for the plan sponsor to solicit detailed information about candidate 401(k) vendors and receive information back from them in a way, which allows the plan sponsor to prepare a side-by-side comparison. Plan sponsors can develop an RFP for their plan. You could supply a sample or they can hire a search consultant to develop the RFP to receive and compare responses from the candidate 401(k) vendors.

If you supply the same sample RFP to 401(k) prospects, both you and the 401(k) vendor(s) you represent will have standardized and refined responses over time.

With an RFP, plan sponsors can better assure that issues particular to their company 401(k) plan and qualities of a 401(k) vendor can be united for the benefit of the company and plan participants. As the RFP is being answered by the 401(k) vendor(s), make sure that you have an opportunity to insert information about yourself, team members and the value-added services you provide to any applicable questions in the RFP.

How do you build your 401(k) sales presentation?

There are four essential segments to a 401(k) sales presentation:

1. **Bridging Back:** restating previous profiling information and confirming plan sponsor and plan participant goals.
2. **Recommendation:** statement of specific solutions to accomplish plan sponsor and plan participant goals.
3. **Analysis:** compare and contrast current, proposed and competing vendors.
4. **Implementation:** schedule of events to effectively install and maintain an optimal 401(k) plan.

Every member of your team should participate in the sales presentation. Your sales presentation provides an opportunity to demonstrate how your recommendation can enhance the prospect 401(k) plan.

Illustrate your partnership with the company during the sales presentation. Purchase a digital camera and insert pictures of their facilities and employees in your presentation.

Who will you present to?

You will be presenting to those people who you have acquired profiling information from during initial profiling and discovery meetings, and additional 401(k) plan decision-makers (their corporate titles may be CEO, president, CFO, and director of human resources). You may also

Presenting Solutions: Effectively communicating
your value and solutions

be presenting to "outside" sources of influence, like attorneys, CPAs and other trusted advisors including employees of the company. Be diligent in your attempt to meet with, or at minimum have a discussion with, all decision-makers prior to your presentation. If you do not accomplish this, you do not know their goals! They may be completely different than your contacts' goals.

A growing number of companies are forming committees made-up of all employee groups to decide who services the company 401(k) plan, instead of the decision being made by one individual.

What should you present during the sales presentation?

Present information that is most important to the 401(k) plan decision-makers. You will know what is important to the decision-makers as a result of questioning them during the discovery meeting. Demonstrate features of the 401(k) vendor's program and your service points in a way that explains how they will accomplish their goals. Tell the 401(k) plan decision-makers what they want to hear.

Offering a proposal from a 401(k) vendor to the plan sponsor will describe the vendor's program. Proposals rarely position the prioritized features, which are important to the 401(k) plan decision-makers. As you present, do not work from the proposal.

- Present what is important to the decision-makers in the order of their priorities with an executive summary. It is easy to get caught up showing features, which are important to you. Stick with the 401(k) plan decision-makers' priorities.
- Communicate your investment management philosophy. Describe the analytical tools you use to help select and monitor the 401(k) plan investment choices. Explain to the 401(k) plan decision-makers how you will help them select and monitor the plan investment choices with a written investment policy.
- Present what your value-added support of the 401(k) plan

will be, i.e., local relationship management and employee retirement education. Help the 401(k) plan decision-makers understand what you will do for them in addition to what the 401(k) vendor will do.

What should you say during the sales presentation?

You can acquire the prospect 401(k) plan by presenting valuable investment options and an efficient operating program. In addition, if you can deliver committed service to the plan and communicate how you will help the 401(k) plan sponsor accomplish his corporate goals for creating this employee benefit plan, you will likely retain the company 401(k) plan.

Tell the 401(k) plan decision-makers how you will talk to their employees; listening to them and answering their questions. Inform the decision-makers that you use hard copy, video and software to reinforce your discussions with employees. Yet you do not let these mediums serve as the primary source of information concerning the 401(k) plan with the employees. **Emphasize that you interpret information for the plan participants and teach them how to use information to prudently accumulate and manage what could be the single largest pool of wealth that they will acquire.** If you are able to interview several current plan participants, ask them their impressions of the plan, changes that they would make and what features are important to them. Then use this information during the sales presentation. Though the 401(k) decision-maker(s) likely knows this, tell him that you believe that employees who feel good about the company benefits will be more loyal and productive. **Let the decision-makers know that you will wave the company flag, while you help the employees realize what a great benefit the 401(k) plan is and that the company is implementing or enhancing the plan for them.** When you refer to employee communications, tell them you combine the resources of your employer, the 401(k) vendor (if different) with your focused retirement planning wisdom and deliver unparalleled local service.

Remark how you will raise the participation rate and the average deferral percentage, and you will promote an appropriate asset allocation model for the plan. Reinforce the point that you are the employees' Retirement Coach™. You are sincerely interested in helping, and you will support your words with actions.

There has been a consistent evolution of the features that 401(k) vendors supply to 401(k) plan sponsors. Long ago, you could impress the 401(k) decision-makers with glitzy materials, like newsletters and brochures. Then daily valuation with 1-800 access to account information arrived. Multiple mutual fund families and Internet access have grown in popularity. **Through this evolution of enhancements from 401(k) vendors, employers' goals have remained consistent for why they create and maintain the company 401(k) plan — to attract, retain, reward, and motivate quality, productive employees.**

Tell the 401(k) plan decision-makers about your team's collective wisdom. Inform them of your experience working with people in changing market environments. How you have helped them effectively navigate through the changes. **Tell the 401(k) plan decision-makers that the most glaring difference between you and your competition is not daily valuation, outside funds or slick promotional materials. The greatest difference is that you have a passion for the work you do.**

Those 401(k) plan sponsors who have had a 401(k) plan for five to ten years may have dealt with several 401(k) vendors and their programs. Plan sponsors have taught themselves what to look for in a 401(k) vendor. Most 401(k) plan sponsors who have employed multiple 401(k) vendors yearn for one vendor they can retain for years. **Experienced 401(k) plan sponsors are most interested in the integrity and reputation of their 401(k) vendor.** Switching 401(k) vendors is disruptive for employees. Plan sponsors are also looking for integrity from financial sales professionals who will work with their employees over the years. **Tell them that with your team, the same members who sell the plan serve as the local relationship managers and the employees' Retirement Coach™.**

Reinforce how you are committed to providing unparalleled support to their employees. You want to help the plan participants confidently build retirement wealth, and you look forward to serving their needs.

How do you open your sales presentation?

A sample sales presentation beginning might sound like this:

"As a way of beginning, I would like each of us in this room to introduce ourselves (again) and briefly state what our responsibilities are to the ABC Company 401(k) plan. My name is _____ and I am responsible for your total satisfaction with our recommended 401(k) program. In addition, I am the lead Retirement Coach™ for your employees, responsible for helping them to confidently use the company 401(k) plan."

Motion for the next team member or 401(k) plan decision-maker to introduce themselves. Once introductions are completed, make the following statement:

"We have a prepared presentation based on information gathered over numerous conversations. Yet we want to make sure we discuss topics which are important to you. Would you please tell us what will be important for you to hear from us today?"

This is an important question to ask because you may have only interviewed one of multiple decision-makers who are now assembled in the meeting. Of course, you have prepared your presentation, yet giving the other decision-makers the opportunity to comment, and the fact that you opened the topic up for discussion in the first place can positively position you.

Other thoughts and exhibits to deliver during the Sales Presentation:

- Make the presentation interactive by asking for feedback from the plan decision-makers throughout.
- Describe your expertise in investments.
- Deliver biographies from all team members.
- Describe your business strategy - how you spend your day.
- Explain what you will do for the plan sponsor, the plan participants, as well as what you do for all of your clients.
- Demonstrate the programs you use to help your clients plan their finances.

SALES 11 IDEA

Consider having a sweatshirt made which says on the front, 401(k) Answer Guy and on the back, Ask Me Your 401(k) Questions! Incorporate the company logo. This idea may sound corny, yet it can demonstrate to the plan decision-makers your uniqueness and desire to have the employees understand that you are responsible to help them to confidently use the company 401(k) plan. Put on the sweatshirt as you describe your educational services to the plan decision-makers.

How can you use comparative matrixes during the sales presentation?

Using comparative matrixes during the sales presentation can provide several benefits for you.

- It demonstrates your consultative role to the decision-makers.
- If you are able to represent multiple 401(k) vendor programs, you can effectively remove any competitors that are able to show the same 401(k) vendor programs.
- You can identify the pros and cons of prospective programs versus the current program.
- Illustrate the investment performance and management fees

of the current or competing investments versus your solution.

- Offer cost savings and effectively eliminate a bid from the company's present 401(k) vendor or competing vendor.

How do you conduct a sales presentation to the plan participants?

A growing trend is the direct involvement of employees in deciding who the company 401(k) vendor will be. For many employers, this has long been a normal part of the company's decision-making process. Other employers will bow to pressure from employees and let the workers be involved as their average 401(k) account balance grows. Encourage this. Do not dissuade the employer from including the employees. We have won seemingly countless plans by communicating to the employees what we will do for them. Employees want to hear the program's features and how you will help them to confidently build their retirement wealth. Deliver a presentation that encompasses many of the exhibits and messages relayed in your employee retirement education meetings.

Tell the plan participants how you will help them set and reach their retirement savings goals by developing appropriate investment strategies and consistently increase their comprehension of investment management.

As their Retirement Coach™, you will listen to them, inform them, answer their questions, interpret information, and help them achieve their goals. Make the employees aware that their 401(k) program will be enhanced. They will be able to more easily access information about their account and the investment choices that are provided in the plan.

Convince them that they can accumulate the single largest pool of wealth by effectively using the company 401(k) plan. Tell them that your guidance and knowledge can help them confidently manage their

*Presenting Solutions: Effectively communicating
your value and solutions*

wealth. **Remember that you are the employees' partner. Let them know you are responsible for helping them establish and accomplish their retirement savings goals.** You will meet with them in a group setting and one-on-one to discuss their investments, the economy and other topics.

What should the 401(k) vendor wholesaler and/or other 401(k) vendor representatives present?

The wholesaler and other company representatives from the 401(k) vendor should present their respective company's program. They should be prepared to answer all program-specific questions posed by 401(k) plan decision-makers and you. **If you allow the 401(k) vendor wholesaler to speak about what you will deliver, local relationship management and employee retirement education services, you will create uncertainty among the 401(k) plan decision-makers as to your ability and desire.** Make sure that you meet to discuss your goals and the meeting's agenda with the 401(k) vendor wholesaler. Coach the 401(k) vendor wholesaler about the role you want them to take during the sales presentation. Make a "dry-run" of the sales presentation to enhance the effectiveness of your message to decision-makers.

What should you listen for during the sales presentation?

Listen to what the decision-makers are telling you. Are they expressing appreciation? Are they telling you that your program is superior to others they have seen, or expressing no opinion? Are they giving buying signals? Are they stating, "When we go with your program, what will happen first?" Are they expressing uncertainty by asking, "How would we transmit payroll information again?"

If the decision-makers are not giving you any opinions or buying signals, ask them questions like:

> *"How do you like the program so far?"* or *"Are we addressing your issues and needs for the company's 401(k) program?"*

How should you respond to questions and/or objections by the decision-makers?

Respond to questions and/or objections in the same manner you would in the prospecting process-directly. Here are some favorite objections, questions and answers:

Objection: "Your costs are too high."
Answer: The best teams in Major League Baseball make the playoffs. Almost every one of the teams is among the top 10 payrolls in the game. In most cases, you get what you pay for. In fact, you will find that our costs are comparable with other 401(k) vendors, yet you will receive greater service from us.

Objection: "Internal investment management fees are too high."
Answer: All returns are net of investment management fees. If one of our recommended funds out-performs on a net basis a lower fee fund of a competitor, is that still a concern?

Question: "How much will you be paid?"
Answer: I am paid X% based on contributions to the plan and X% on the growth of total plan assets. As the plan participants prosper, I prosper. As the plan participants suffer, I suffer.

When should you go for the close?

When you believe the time is right, ask for the order. Use your best judgment. After you complete the sales presentation, and you have

Presenting Solutions: Effectively communicating your value and solutions

answered all questions, re-emphasize your ability to service the 401(k) plan. Tell them you look forward to working for them and with the plan participants.

Here are two actual closing statements from previous presentations:

SALES 12 IDEA

"This is not only the 401(k) plan for ABC Company, this is the primary retirement wealth accumulation vehicle for each of your employees. We believe that the XYZ 401(k) program will best help you to accomplish your corporate goals for creating and maintaining the 401(k) plan. In addition, we believe that our role of working with your employees will help them to confidently use this "tool" you have provided for them to effectively accumulate and manage their retirement wealth. Where do we go from here?"

This close was used when we were absolutely certain of the pay-out on the mutual funds currently being used by the prospective 401(k) plan:

SALES 13 IDEA

"Your current 401(k) plan uses mutual funds. The class of mutual funds your plan is using pays a trailer commission of .25% on the total dollars invested in the funds and 1% on all new contributions to your broker. The plan has $5 million currently with annual contributions of $1 million invested in the mutual funds. Your current broker is being paid $12,500 a year in trailer commissions and $10,000 in commissions from new contributions, for a total of $22,500. Comparing the amount of benefit your broker is providing to the plan and the plan participants, is it the same level that a typical $22,500 a year employee at your company produces? We want to go to work for the company and your employees. What can we do to earn the job?"

What are some effective follow-up techniques to the 401(k) plan decision-makers after the sales presentation(s)?

Your prospect has completed a long sales process with you and your competitors. Though you have offered extensive and clear details, making a decision is still imposing, especially if they are not familiar or comfortable with 401(k) plan decisions.

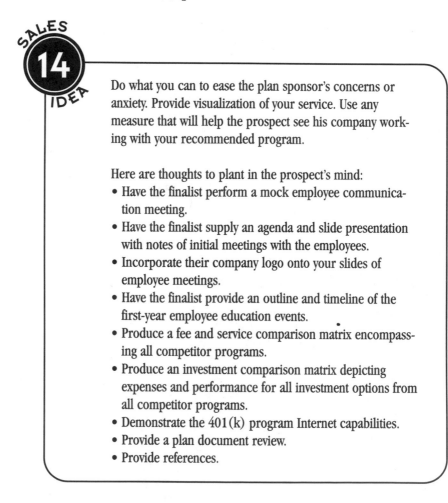

SALES 14 IDEA

Do what you can to ease the plan sponsor's concerns or anxiety. Provide visualization of your service. Use any measure that will help the prospect see his company working with your recommended program.

Here are thoughts to plant in the prospect's mind:
- Have the finalist perform a mock employee communication meeting.
- Have the finalist supply an agenda and slide presentation with notes of initial meetings with the employees.
- Incorporate their company logo onto your slides of employee meetings.
- Have the finalist provide an outline and timeline of the first-year employee education events.
- Produce a fee and service comparison matrix encompassing all competitor programs.
- Produce an investment comparison matrix depicting expenses and performance for all investment options from all competitor programs.
- Demonstrate the 401(k) program Internet capabilities.
- Provide a plan document review.
- Provide references.

Presenting Solutions: Effectively communicating
your value and solutions

How do you manage the time between proposals and closing the sale?

Time will lapse between presenting your recommendations and being chosen. The plan sponsor may have to interview additional bidders. Maybe members of the 401(k) committee, who determine the future vendor(s) of the plan are traveling. Or perhaps they are tackling corporate deadlines. There are many reasons that time — sometimes significant time — passes between the first presentation, the second, the third, and so on.

Assume your competitors are not passively waiting. You should keep your name in front of the 401(k) plan decision-maker(s) via letter, demonstration software or personal visit. Show the prospect that you are an effective communicator and are interested in serving the company 401(k) plan.

Send a summation letter to the 401(k) plan decision-makers. This letter will reinforce main points explained during the sales presentation. A sample of a summation letter follows on the next page. Please have your office Compliance Officer review any outgoing correspondence before sending.

Dear ABC Company 401(k) Plan Decision-Maker,

We want to take this time to reinforce that when we are chosen to enhance the ABC Company 401(k) plan, there will be several organizational details to complete to implement an efficient and successful conversion.

XYZ 401(k) vendor organization will be responsible for working with you and the current recordkeeper to transfer and transmit plan data. Our local team will work with you and XYZ 401(k) vendor to construct and deliver an effective employee education campaign.

Here is a suggested timeline that we have found successful in implementing and managing the communication process for the plan participants:

January 1 - Send employees a letter from the CEO announcing plan changes and alert them of upcoming presentation dates.
January 2 - Display posters and include first payroll stuffer with payroll checks.
January 9 - Include second payroll stuffer with payroll checks.
January 16 - Include third payroll stuffer with payroll checks.
January 20 - Conduct transition meeting (conversion plan only).
January 27 - Conduct enrollment meeting.
February 28 - Conduct "Update" meeting (conversion plan only).
March 15 - Conduct "Go Live" meeting (conversion plan only).
April 27 - Conduct re-enrollment and update meeting.

We will be calling soon to discuss this timeline and to answer any questions you have. Thank you again for the opportunity to compete to enhance the ABC Company 401(k) plan. We look forward to working with you and the plan participants.

Sincerely,

Your Name Here

Presenting Solutions: Effectively communicating
your value and solutions

Also consider offering assistance to the 401(k) plan decision-maker(s) in comparing the 401(k) vendor competitors from a fee, service and investment management perspective. The Department of Labor Fee Comparison Worksheet is a great tool for doing this. You will find the form in the Appendix in Exhibit #4 or you can obtain a copy by going to the Department of Labor web site at www.dol.gov/PWBA.

Supply blank comparison matrixes or insist that you and your team do the work. You not only gain by demonstrating a valuable service to the 401(k plan decision-maker(s); you will also gain valuable information about your competitors.

What do you do when you win the 401(k) plan?

Once you are chosen, the acquisition activities end and retention strategies begin. Starting the relationship with effective support, and doing what you said you would do through the acquisition phase with the 401(k) plan decision-makers, will impact the quality and duration of the retention of the relationship. When the hunt is over and you are the winner, thank the plan sponsor in writing and schedule the "welcome" conference call.

Remember buyer remorse. Reinforce what a great decision they made to choose you to manage the 401(k) plan. Disgruntled competitors may attempt cheap shots at you. Install a "force field" and act quickly to implement the program. Take control over the implementation process. There are five parts to a 401(k) plan; the plan document, plan administration, investment management, employee retirement education, and trust services. All five disciplines need to be addressed during start-up services. Schedule a "welcome" conference call with all interested parties, including the plan sponsor, the 401(k) vendor company operational representatives and you.

There are four partners in a 401(k) plan; the plan sponsor, the plan participants, the 401(k) vendor, and you, the financial sales profession-al. Each partner has roles and responsibilities to understand and exe-cute during the implementation process and you are the quarterback. In a conversion plan there is a fifth partner, the current 401(k) vendor. They must efficiently perform their duties to provide a final plan valua-tion and communicate all outstanding issues in order for a timely con-version to take place.

401(k) Sales Champion™

Stay involved with the start-up services. Your job during the conversion is to make sure that your client, the plan sponsor, is getting the attention they need from the 401(k) vendor. Make sure the plan sponsor is getting the service promised by the 401(k) vendor during the sales presentations.

"Crow" when you win. If the plan sponsor agrees, run a compliance-approved ad in a local paper or web site to announce that your organization is pleased to have been chosen to service their company 401(k) plan. You can also send out a compliance- and client-approved press release to be placed in the media. It's not only great publicity for you, but also for the plan sponsor to be known to have hired such a quality organization. Plan sponsors will want all current and potential employees to know what a great benefit they have to look forward to.

What occurs operationally during a conversion?

Conversions occur only with existing 401(k) plans when they transfer from the "old" to the "new" 401(k) vendor(s). The act of conversion can affect all five parts of the 401(k), yet most attention is given to the plan investments and plan administration components.

A conversion date will be determined by the new 401(k) vendor(s) and the plan sponsor. Typically, the new 401(k) vendor will set a conversion date for 60 business days after being awarded the plan. As an example, say your client wants to begin a relationship with a new 401(k) program vendor January 1. Your client will have had to choose the new vendor by the previous October 1 in order to comply with the new vendor's time requirements. All too often financial sales professionals try to "push" for a shorter time period, yet you should let the vendor determine what they can deliver. 401(k) vendors determine their timeframe on their best practices. Encouraging them to "work harder" may actually leave some service issues unattended. Enough time has to be established to set up the new plan document, chose the investments, schedule and conduct initial employee education events and transfer existing plan data.

If the existing plan assets are going to transfer to a new 401(k) vendor, they can be transferred in one of two ways; a cash or a mapping conversion. With a cash conversion of the plan assets, the investments are liquidated on the last business day the markets are opened prior to the conversion date. The cash balances are invested in a money market account, earning interest for the plan participants, and once the conversion is complete, plan participants can then invest those cash balances into their selection of investment choices. With a mapping conversion, a like-fund alignment is established with the new investment, e.g. large-cap growth fund to large-cap growth fund. On the last business day before the conversion date the current investments are liquidated. Once settlement occurs, the cash is then invested into the like-fund from which it came for each respective plan participant, instead of being invested in a money market fund. Like fund plan asset transfer, also known as mapping, is the method most often used to move money to a new 401(k) vendor. The reason why mapping transfer of plan assets is preferred is because with a cash conversion the "old" money assets are not out-of-the-market during conversion. You see with a conversion there is "old" money, which are the current assets and "new" money, which are current and ongoing contributions.

"Old" and "new" money... now that brings up the other primary aspect of conversion; tranferring the plan data from the current 401(k) plan administrator vendor to the new one. The sooner the old data is sent to and reconciled by the new plan administration vendor, the sooner plan participants can access information and, transact their account with the new 401(k) vendor. The time period that plan participants cannot access information and fully transact their account, take loans or other distributions and fully transact their account is affectionately known as the "black-out" period. The duration of the "black-out" period is ultimately determined by the amount of time the old vendor takes in delivering old data to the new vendor, and then how long it takes the new vendor to reconcile, or make sure that the data is accurate, then joining the old data with the new data acquired by the new 401(k) vendor following the conversion date. Once the old data has been reconciled and joined with the new data, the plan is "live" and full functionality for access to account information and transactions by the plan participants can take place.

Allow the wholesaler and other administration representatives of the "new" 401(k) vendor(s) to explain their process to you. You will have to make sure that the plan sponsor and plan participants understand the timeline for changing and how long it could take. "What's the man doing with the money?" will be a phrase you will hear from frustrated plan participants as a result of their inability to access information about their 401(k) account. Your ability to inform and educate them will go a long way in lessening their frustration.

MARKETPLACE FACT 27

Blackout Periods Just Got Shorter:

MassMutual Retirement Services, which completed the industry's first weekend blackout conversion for a 401(k) plan last fall, has completed a midweek, overnight conversion for 401(k) client Mount Kisco Medical Group, P.C., a plan with $35 million in assets and 320 participants. Mass Mutual's conversion for Mount Kisco began on a late Tuesday afternoon when Mount Kisco's particpant records were received (assets were transferred eight days earlier). In less than 24 hours, the entire plan's participant records– including loan records–were built on MassMutual's System and ready for use.

Source: IOMA, August 2000

What are the basic musts
for a "welcome" conference call?

During the "welcome" conference call with the plan sponsor, 401(k) vendor and yourself, discuss roles, responsibilities and what needs to be done when and by whom during the implementation phase.

After you finish the "welcome" call, the 401(k) vendor's operational representatives should publish an implementation timeline, which outlines roles, responsibilities and deadlines. The implementation timeline consists of activity definition, which permits process management by you.

Send letters to all 401(k) vendor and company representatives who participated in the "welcome" call. Thank them for their time and knowledge. This may seem like a minor act, but it will pave a path to smooth relationships and lead to support when you need it.

What are the various types of employee
retirement education meetings?

There are potentially six types of employee retirement education meetings.

1. **Transition:** Delivered only with a conversion plan. The purpose is to communicate to the employees the reason and process of changing 401(k) vendors.

2. **Initial:** Delivered with a start-up plan. The purpose is to raise awareness among employees of the 401(k) plan.

3. **Enrollment:** Delivered with start-up and conversion plans. The purpose is to discuss the need to use the 401(k), the rules of

the plan, investment choices, investment management topics such as asset allocation and dollar cost averaging, as well as enrollment instructions.

4. **Update:** Delivered only with a conversion plan. The purpose is to inform the plan participants about the progress of completing the conversion process. Update the plan participants with information about where we were, where we are and where we are going with the conversion process.

5. **"Go Live":** Delivered only with a conversion plan. The purpose is to welcome the plan participants to the full access of information by demonstrating the Voice Response System (VRU), Internet and delivery of first participant statements (if applicable).

6. **Ongoing:** Delivered with start-up and conversion plans. The purpose is to reinforce investment management topics as well as inform plan participants of changes which affect their 401(k) plan and the accumulation of their retirement wealth.

Who at the company should be involved with the development of employee retirement education events?

Your 401(k) vendor should be able to supply you with all your employee education event materials, including payroll stuffers, posters, presentations, and even door prizes.

Anyone at the company who normally schedules, plans and conducts employee meetings, as well as representatives from the 401(k) vendor and you will be involved in the development of events for the employees.

If possible, obtain an employee database with home mailing addresses so that you can send out a follow-up letter after the enrollment meeting. The mailing list will also provide a database to enhance your ability to efficiently deliver future plan information as well as aid you with your cross-selling marketing efforts. **Be sensitive to those employers who may not understand the benefit of you having the employees' home addresses. Do not insist that the employer provide them to you. The follow-up letter contains the major points discussed about the 401(k) plan and recites the most salient questions with answers asked by employees during the enrollment meeting.**

When should you schedule enrollment meetings?

Enrollment meetings should be scheduled at a time when the most eligible employees can attend. Tell the employer about the importance of every employee hearing about the 401(k) plan details. Some employers invite the spouses of their employees to attend enrollment meetings. In these cases, the meetings will likely be held after business hours.

Employers will tell you how and when they have had the best success with employee meetings. Make sure to ask the employer for their advice regarding the day of week and time of day to hold the meetings.

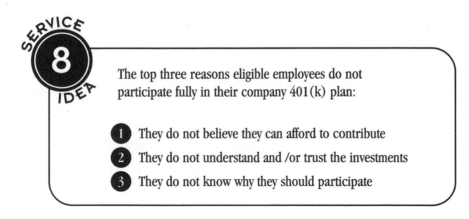

SERVICE 8 IDEA

The top three reasons eligible employees do not participate fully in their company 401(k) plan:

1 They do not believe they can afford to contribute
2 They do not understand and /or trust the investments
3 They do not know why they should participate

Some employers will hesitate to make the enrollment meeting mandatory, meaning the employees are paid to attend on company time. Be adamant that all eligible employees attend the enrollment meeting. **Explain to those employers that mandatory attendance is the best way to assure that they get what they are paying for and that the employees receive the education they deserve.**

Some employees may be hesitant to attend the enrollment meetings. You will be surprised how even those folks can be coaxed with door prizes. Ask the 401(k) vendor wholesaler for some door prize incentives.

Is there any difference in the enrollment meeting between a start-up and a conversion plan?

With a start-up plan, every employee is at the same place — learning about the plan and how to enroll. With a conversion plan you may want to segregate the employees into those who currently participate and those eligible, non-participating employees. For those who participated in the old plan, you may want to focus on transition issues. For those who did not previously participate, discuss why they should be involved in the new plan.

Of course, the encouragement a current participant can offer an eligible, non-participating employee can be valuable. Having both groups together in one meeting can be beneficial. Discuss this with the plan sponsor.

Selling a 401(k) plan to employees

Regardless of the investment sophistication of the employees, it is a good idea to remind everyone of the basics of the 401(k) plan and investing. Professional athletes practice the basics continually. Perhaps you open by talking about the harsh reality of retirement planning.

Most retirees do not have adequate retirement savings and have no choice but to live on less money. And it is not certain how long Social Security will exist in its current structure of benefits. Of course, the typical Social Security check does not provide the same financial comfort of a regular paycheck.

After addressing the importance of retirement planning, quickly move to a more positive and motivating subject. Explain to employees how, with a 401(k) plan, they can begin building their financial security. The 401(k) plan can help plan participants accumulate the single largest pool of wealth they will likely save and manage in their lives.

How you explain a 401(k) plan to an employee depends upon the level of investment sophistication they possess. You will communicate best to the majority of employees when you explain concepts in terms that they can understand. Some employees have participated in previous employer 401(k) plans and/or invested on their own for years. Many employees are less sophisticated or first-time investors. They will not be familiar with standard industry jargon, so clarity is crucial.

For less sophisticated employees, begin by telling them how their employer established the plan to help them save for their future. Using payroll deduction, the dollars they designate are withdrawn from their paycheck and placed in the their own account. **Plan participants should focus on saving a percentage of their earnings instead of a specific dollar amount.** By saving a percentage of earnings the plan participant's savings will rise or fall depending on how much they earn. Many do not change the dollar amount of their savings and find that, as their incomes rise, the percent they save for retirement actually declines. Saving a percentage of what they earn allows plan participants' contributions to keep pace with their increased earnings. As they receive future bonuses and raises, plan participants' actual savings will keep pace with their increasing standard of living. Being able to maintain their same spending habits in retirement should be a primary goal for plan participants. Importantly, some employers match the employee's contribution. Essentially, this is "free" money for a participating employee. If there is a company match in a 401(k) plan, participants achieve greater savings for their retirement goal! **The minimum an employee should contribute to their account is the maximum amount the employer matches.**

A primary reason why eligible employees do not participate in their company 401(k) plan is the fear of receiving less money from their paycheck. There are significant tax advantages with a 401(k) plan. If a participant saves $1.00 in a 401(k) plan, he does not actually take home $1.00 less in his paycheck. Instead, he may take home between $.65 to $.85 less, depending on the participant's tax bracket because of federal, and, in most cases, state income tax savings.

Perhaps one of the most beneficial aspects of a 401(k) plan is the cost to plan participants. A 401(k) plan is usually one of the least expensive "tools" a plan participant can use to accumulate retirement wealth. There is usually investment management expense and perhaps a small dollar amount to cover their share of plan administration expense. Yet when compared to an IRA or savings account, the benefits far outweigh any costs paid by the plan participant.

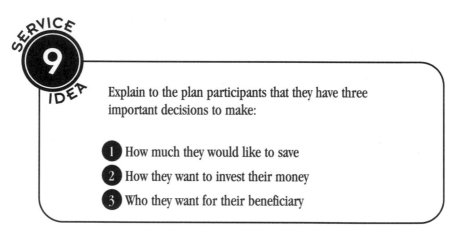

Explain to the plan participants that they have three important decisions to make:

1 How much they would like to save

2 How they want to invest their money

3 Who they want for their beneficiary

Ted Benna notes from his experience in talking to 401(k) participants that the automatic saving which occurs through payroll deduction is the most valuable benefit of a 401(k) plan. 401(k) plans convert employees from spenders to savers, by making saving their first priority. Many employees need this automated saving through payroll deduction.

What should you not talk about during the enrollment meeting?

Do not talk about how you can help the plan participants with other aspects of their financial life. Save that discussion for those who ask for your assistance and meet with them individually after the enrollment meeting. **Plan sponsors do not want to feel as if they have opened the door to a financial product "pusher."** Stay focused on the 401(k) plan and promote its use.

Do not use industry jargon. Be conscious of what you are saying and to whom you are speaking. **The rapport you hope to build with the employees can be enhanced if they understand what you are saying to them.**

What are some questions most often asked by employees during the enrollment meetings?

You will be asked every question imaginable about IRAs, Roth IRAs and IRA roll-overs. Become an expert in this. The information is not difficult and your quick and confident answer will build trust.

Question: Is my money safe if something happens to the company?
Answer: Yes. Your money is held in trust, segregated from company assets.

Question: How much is this going to cost me?
Answer: (If the employer is paying out-of-pocket expenses) "You pay nothing out of your pocket for this benefit. There is a cost to you though and it is an opportunity lost cost. It is fair to state that if you do not save for your retirement years through a program like a 401(k), you will probably live in retirement dependent upon family, friends and the government. You will have missed the opportunity to be independent in your retirement years."

Question: How much should I invest?

Answer:: We may have to address that one-on-one. We will be completing a worksheet momentarily to help you determine the amount of your savings. You may want to consider saving at least as much as the match formula so you can get the maximum employer contribution (if an employer match contribution is offered). Most of us do not save enough, and we should all save as much as we can. Maybe your goal should be to retire with too much money.

Question: What will be the impact on my paycheck?

Answer: There will be an impact, but it will be less than what you are saving. As an example, if you save $10, your paycheck may only be $8.50 less because you have paid less in taxes.

Question: How should I invest my money?

Answer:: We will go through an asset allocation exercise, which will help you understand how to invest your money. If you still have questions after the exercise, I would like to meet with you individually.

Question: Who should I name as my beneficiary?

Answer: If you are married, your spouse will be your beneficiary unless they agree in writing not to be. If you are not married, you can name any individual or organization.

Why are off-site educational events effective?

Some employers may not want ongoing employee retirement education events conducted at their business, believing the meeting could impact company production. Holding off-site educational events can alleviate this concern yet still offer ongoing educational support necessary to help the plan sponsor accomplish their corporate goals while giving the plan participants the information they need. Off-site educational events allow you to strengthen your relationships with plan participants while not hampering production at the employer's workplace. If you conduct educational events off-site, you will be building relationships with the employees away from the workplace. It is a win-win situation for all involved.

How do you conduct employee education events in remote company locations?

If travel to a remote company location is prohibitive, videotape the enrollment meeting at the main facility and provide copies to the remote location. Another option is to arrange a conference call or live webcast where all participants can be involved. If all else fails there is always the old-fashioned way of simply contacting employees one at a time.

Spending time with each employee at remote locations is just as essential as it is with the employees at the main facility. This is a great reason to have in place a regional/national team or network of fellow financial sales professionals.

Managers of remote locations often travel to the main facility. When they do, make sure you meet with them and help them understand the 401(k) program. Train the trainer. Then they can best communicate plan provisions to the employees.

How do you retain your 401(k) plans?

Deliver the type of service you promised. Always think of ways to serve more effectively and you will retain your 401(k) plans. **Providing value-added service will enhance your probability of retaining the 401(k) plan.**

As time goes on, 401(k) vendors will employ better technology and processes, which will allow them to lower the fees they charge. 401(k) vendors may even start to give away frequent flyer miles. **Keep your services the same and you will be caught up in the "price war" marketplace. Raise your value-added services over time and you will be less vulnerable to marketplace pricing issues.**

Value added services could include:

- Return all phone calls, e-mails and other inquiries from the employer and employees the same day.
- Annual reviews with plan trustees concerning investments and employee education events for the company.
- Plan periodic programs conducted to help plan sponsors stay abreast of 401(k) marketplace changes.
- Produce an annual survey of employees polling their perceptions of the company 401(k) plan and eliciting enhancement suggestions from them.
- Produce an annual survey of the local employers concerning their company retirement plan offerings.
- Hold quarterly retirement education workshops and enrollment meetings for the employees.

Do not hesitate to inform plan sponsor clients of better 401(k) programs in the marketplace. You will be their trusted advisor, and you can reduce your competition by keeping your client informed. **If you become indispensable to both the employer and the employees, you will retain the company 401(k) plan.**

Why is ongoing service important?

In order for you to receive maximum benefit from the company 401(k) plan, you must retain it. Ongoing service is important because you will remind the decision-makers why they chose you to service the company 401(k) plan. Ongoing service is also important because companies merge, and decision-makers change companies. You want to secure your position with the company and decision-makers as a 401(k) Sales Champion™.

Remaining in front of the trustees and plan participants, effectively communicating useful investment and retirement information, is your key to developing long-term relationships with the decision-makers and employees.

As 401(k) plan assets grow, the question becomes whether you, as the financial sales professional, remain to enjoy the growth of those assets and the relationships with the plan participants. The plan assets will take care of themselves. Efficiently managing the plan participants is critical. Ask yourself continually, "Am I effectively helping the trustees manage their fiduciary responsibilities and plan participants to build up their individual assets, enhancing retention of the relationship, and permitting cross-selling opportunities?"

How do you manage your time as your practice grows?

As your practice grows, quarterly education events and one-on-one meetings in your office may not be practical. Consider semi-annual or annual education events. Spend a whole day at the company and have one-on-one meetings there. You can easily assist participants in 10 to 20 minutes. The participants who need more help or have other assets to discuss may set a time to come to see you.

Certain plans may be more advantageous to spend time with. A doctor's group, law firm, or other professional organizations may be brimming with prospects. Do not hesitate to see them quarterly.

What do you talk about at ongoing employee retirement education meetings?

Use your firm's, the 401(k) vendor's, or independent source's research pieces. Talk to the employees about past performance of the markets and future prognostications. Remind participants about the principals of enrollment and investment management. Talk to them about additional financial goals like college funding, tax reduction and home ownership. Pick a main topic and keep the discussion within 30 minutes. Be available to meet with employees individually after the group meeting. This can establish substantial cross-selling opportunities for you.

Be prepared with a presentation on market volatility. Call the plan sponsor to schedule the meeting whenever markets are abnormally volatile.

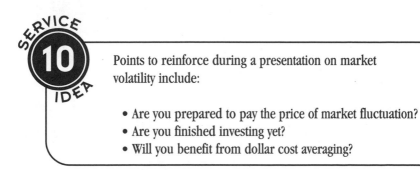

Points to reinforce during a presentation on market volatility include:

- Are you prepared to pay the price of market fluctuation?
- Are you finished investing yet?
- Will you benefit from dollar cost averaging?

How can you develop cross-selling strategies for the plan sponsor and plan participants?

Annually, send the plan sponsor a note that reads: Please tell me how our team (or I) can improve our service to you and your employees. We want to help your employees better understand the benefit of the 401(k) plan, and the value of their employment at ABC Company.

Sincerely,
(Your Name Here)

Stay in communication with the plan sponsor. Through ongoing conversations, you will discover needs the organization has. After-tax savings, deferred compensation, cash management, and lines of credit are some of the potential cross-selling opportunities with plan sponsors. Obtain a mailing list of plan participants and update it annually. Mail a follow-up letter to them after each meeting with them. Offer plan participants a one-on-one annual review at your office. Some financial service companies have free or low-cost financial planning programs. Offer the plan participants the financial planning program.

As you provide ongoing retirement and investment education to plan participants, you develop an expert reputation. Interested employees will inevitably approach you, and request that you help them manage an IRA or recommend avenues to help them save money for other goals like their child's college education.

Hold off-site educational meetings with plan participants, spouses and their guests, and speak about a variety of investment subjects. You will have a captive audience – plan participants – who already know you are concerned about their future wealth. Let the plan participants know that you can assist them at distribution time as well. **You want to capture their rollover! All your hard work will be wasted it you don't!**

How can you assist plan participants and build relationships with them?

Service them. Let them know that you care about them. Return phone calls and other inquiries quickly and answer questions so plan participants can understand your answer.

Give each plan participant a three-ring binder. The cover will have the name of the plan, company name and logo, along with your name and phone number. Here they can keep the summary plan description, two or three years' worth of statements, any worksheets that you provide to help them to understand how much they should save and how to invest their money. This can facilitate annual reviews you have with the plan participants.

These are the documents employers must provide to employees upon request:

- Form 5500 or Form 5500-C/R
- The summary plan description
- The plan document
- The trust agreement setting up the plan, if separate from the plan
- Any collective bargaining contract, if appropriate
- Any other instrument under which the plan was established or is operated

Make all requests for plan documents in writing. If the administrator fails to give you information you are entitled to within 30 days of your written request, and the reasons

continues to next page

continues from previous page

for the delay are within the administrator's control, you also have the right to bring a lawsuit against the plan administrator, and ask the court to make the plan administrator pay you a fine of up to $100 a day for every day the administrator goes over the 30-day deadline. It is a good idea to send your request by certified mail, return receipt requested, so that you will have a record of when you made the request.

Source: U.S. Department of Labor Pension and Welfare Benefits Administration, PWBA

Schedule a one-on-one meeting with every plan participant to take place at your office or at the company. Encourage the plan participant to bring their spouse. **Send to the plan participant a profiling questionnaire to complete before the meeting takes place.** Let the plan participant know that the purpose of the questionnaire is to help you help them manage their 401(k) account in "concert with" their total net worth.

What are other ways of staying in front of plan participants?

The company may hold an employee work-oriented meeting on occasion. Ask for five to 10 minutes to speak to the employees about the 401(k) plan.

Employees receive raises throughout the year and this is a good time to reinforce the need to save a percentage of their wages instead of a flat dollar amount. Provide to the human resources office a letter to give to each employee that receives a raise. The letter can explain how the employee may be able to save a greater amount for their retirement years.

Produce T-shirts with the company logo on them and the statement, "I'm planning on retiring with too much money because of the (company name) 401(k) plan," and give them to all plan participants.

Contribute to the company quarterly newsletter. Address topics like dollar cost averaging, market volatility and financial planning. Make sure that your phone number and e-mail address is prominently displayed on the newsletter.

Provide the employer with a board to post 401(k) information, with compartments for brochures. Your name, email address and phone number should all be prominently displayed.

How does an employer evaluate investment performance?

Employers can evaluate investment performance by establishing a written investment policy. Within the written investment policy, define benchmarks to compare investment choices against. If the plan is using mutual funds, contact the respective mutual fund company when establishing benchmarks for the respective investment choices. Ask the mutual fund company representative about the benchmark index to which the respective funds are compared against. Each year, ask the mutual fund company to confirm they are using the same benchmark(s). If you learn that the benchmark has changed, investigate further into the fund and determine whether or not to recommend to the plan sponsor to retain the choice.

Provide investment performance of current choices compared against appropriate benchmarks, and if you have an under-performing option, be proactive. Be able to explain the poor performance and advise about replacing or retaining the option or adding investment options.

What are written investment policies?

A written investment policy is a tool for trustees to use in selecting and managing the plan investments. There are varied opinions as to the complexity and completeness necessary to have an effective written investment policy.

A written investment policy could include:

- Company history
- Plan history
- A listing of trustees
- A listing of investment management style categories
- A description of investment categories
- A listing of the actual investments along with a comparative matrix with benchmark for each investment choice
- A discussion of the process to annually review the investment menu
- A discussion of the process to include an investment choice
- A discussion of the process to replace an investment choice

Many 401(k) vendors can supply a written investment policy template. Each trustee should sign the written investment policy. After it is examined each year, a corporate resolution should provide evidence of the review.

A written investment policy is a positive tool for 401(k) plan sponsors and individual investors alike to better communicate and manage investments. You will find a sample written investment policy in the Appendix, Exhibit #5.

How does a plan sponsor evaluate the effectiveness of the total 401(k) program?

Helping the plan sponsor evaluate the effectiveness of the 401(k) program can ensure that the 401(k) plan prospers under your guidance. Establish performance objectives with the plan sponsor, the program vendor and yourself.

Survey the employees each year to determine their overall level of satisfaction and learn about specific likes and dislikes about the program.

Every two years, complete a fee and service worksheet similar to the Department of Labor Fee Comparison Worksheet found in the Appendix, Exhibit #4.

Encourage the plan sponsor to retain copies of all educational materials throughout the year and plan an annual review of educational efforts. Assist the plan sponsor in reviewing the written investment policy to ensure that policy provisions are adhered to. All of these exhibits can be archived within the Plan Sponsor Book (PSB). Helping the plan sponsor to evaluate the effectiveness of the 401(k) program can ensure that the 401(k) plan prospers under your guidance.

How do you help employers manage their fiduciary responsibilities?

Conduct annual reviews with trustees in conjunction with the Plan Sponsor Book (PSB) to review investment management and employee retirement education events. The PSB is a three-ring binder that helps the employer manage his fiduciary responsibilities. The book is a central depository where the plan sponsor maintains exhibits and illustrations that were used to explain retirement education and investment information to the employees.

401(k) Sales Champion™

At a minimum, the PSB could contain a copy of the plan adoption agreement, summary plan description, written investment policy, investment matrix with comparative indices, and all employee communication materials and employee retirement education meeting sign-up sheets.

Plan sponsors will be impressed with the uniqueness and usefulness of the PSB. The plan sponsor will appreciate the PSB as a tool that helps them organize and compile important, fiduciary-based information. The PSB provides a quick reference to past policies and programs and can be used as a review when developing strategies for the company 401(k) plan. Prepare a working paper of past annual goals and objectives for the plan assets and employee education. Discuss results and initiatives for the next year on an annual basis with the employer, using the Annual Review Worksheet found in the Appendix, Exhibit #3.

MARKETPLACE FACT 29

When the DoL informs the plan sponsor of an audit, a form letter is mailed asking to ready copies of the following:

- The plan document and all amendments
- The annual tax return for the plan (IRS Form 5500) for the last 3 years
- The summary annual report provided to participants for the last 3 years
- The summary plan description for the plan, as well as all amendments thereto
- Sample distribution forms provided to participants, so that DoL may determine compliance with the notice, spouse consent, and ERISA joint and survivor annuity requirements
- The fidelity bond for the plan, which is required under ERISA
- The financial statements for the plan
- A list of the plan's investments
- The plan's investment policy
- Minutes of meetings of the trustee or investment committee, which reflect how investment decisions are made

continues to next page

MARKETPLACE FACT 29

continued from previous page

- Information regarding the plan's policies with respect to the voting of proxies

Source: San Antonio Business Journal, May 8, 2000, "Audits ensure retirement plan upholds participants rights," R. Bradley Oxford.

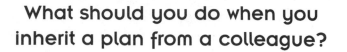

What should you do when you inherit a plan from a colleague?

When you inherit a plan from a colleague, treat the opportunity as a competitive situation and take immediate action. Call and introduce yourself to the plan sponsor. Schedule a personal meeting. Conduct a discovery meeting and learn about your new client. Learn about the 401(k) plan, and the employer's objectives. Provide details of your value-added services, and be sure to demonstrate that you welcome the chance to work with the plan sponsor and his plan participants.

Demonstrate to the plan sponsor that you will provide an upgrade in service to the plan and plan participants. This initial series of contacts could very well resemble prospecting and profiling efforts you would normally accomplish with "cold" prospects. Do not be surprised if the plan sponsor wants to put the plan out for bid as a result of your colleague leaving. You may have to fight to retain the plan.

How do you acquire 401(k) plans as a result of a broker-of-record change?

If your broker/dealer has a sales agreement with the current 401(k) vendor, the trustees of the 401(k) plan can write a letter to the 401(k) vendor and explain that they want their relationship assigned to you. The trustees of the 401(k) program should contact the vendor to determine their specific processes that must be followed to effect a broker-of-record change.

When you gain a 401(k) plan from a broker-of-record change, immediately conduct employee retirement education events. Poor service probably led the plan sponsor to make the broker-of-record change. This is your chance to show the plan sponsor what an ambitious and sincere financial sales professional can do for the plan participants.

You should know that there are plenty of 401(k) plans that do not have any broker-of-record. Speak to 401(k) wholesalers and explain to them that you can help their organization retain those plans without a broker-of-record by delivering exceptional local service. The trustees of the 401(k) plan will have to approve you of course.

How do you work with an employer that does not prefer an ideal 401(k) plan?

Use your business judgment in these cases. If you have a plan sponsor who is not fully concerned about the vitality and effectiveness of the program and they are not interested in ensuring that the plan participants reap the best rewards from the 401(k) plan, consider releasing the client. **Some of you may decide to keep the relationship since you are being paid, even though you may be in an environment that is not conducive for maximizing your compensation potential.** Before ending the client relationship, you may want to conduct a survey with the plan participants sharing their views of the plan. Prepare and deliver a proposal containing participant opinions of the plan and recommendations that will help to convince the plan sponsor that the 401(k) plan needs their support.

What if the plan sponsor does not select you?

No professional baseball player has ever batted .500, and only a handful of players have hit .400. The best hitters bat .300, meaning they succeed three out of every 10 trips to the plate.

Selected Topics

As a financial sales professional, you will not get a hit every time you step to the plate. There will be times plan sponsors choose someone else. Instead of sulking, remember that the time may arrive when the plan is bid again, only the next time it will likely have more assets. Perhaps the decision was difficult, and the plan sponsor will remember you if the chosen financial sales professional does not perform up to standards.

Respond like a 401(k) Sales Champion™. Explain to the decision-maker that you are truly disappointed as you were looking forward to working with this company. Uncover why the decision was made and explain that you will be in the 401(k) plan business for the next 20 years (or however long until you plan to retire) and you look forward to bidding on the plan the next time they review it.

Learn from the experience. Mail a professional acceptance letter, requesting permission to learn why the winner was chosen and why you were not. Include a questionnaire and follow-up the mailing with a call. You have nothing to lose when you ask what led to the decision. Use this defeat to build your credibility for the next attempt to win the plan, and use the experience to learn for the sake of pursuing current and future prospects. If you weren't chosen, yet worked hard, and the plan sponsor realizes your effort, he will want you to be rewarded. Stop by with 20 IRA rollover kits with a note, which might read:

"Although we were unsuccessful in earning the opportunity to service the ABC company 401(k) plan, I would still like to help plan participants when they take a distribution. This is a large part of my business. Please distribute these kits to employees who are receiving a distribution from the plan."

Remove the company from the hot prospect file and return it to the cold prospect file. Continue follow-up communication with the company, just as you did before it became a hot prospect. **Do not insult the plan sponsor by "bad mouthing" the winner.** You may feel like degrading their decision, but you will not enhance your reputation with your sour feelings. You do not want to burn bridges, especially since the opportunity may arise again to pursue the plan sponsor's business. The next time you call on that company, you will know better what the plan sponsor is looking for, and how to show that you can provide the plan sponsor the services and features he desires. **Remember to ask for referrals.** This will show that you are truly a professional, and you are sincerely interested in providing service to the 401(k) marketplace in your community.

Remember the positives instead of dwelling on the negatives when you do not win a plan. When the plan is bid again due to a lack of service, you will not be the professional responsible. Also, you will have one less competitor at the table, and the plan will be larger. You may have also discovered other financial product sale opportunities, like cash management or deferred compensation, through the prospecting and sales processes. Ask the plan sponsor if they want to pursue solutions to those corporate needs.

After a year has passed, send the plan sponsor a note, which mentions the anniversary of the decision to choose the current vendor. Tell the decision-makers that, if they are not pleased with the present vendor's performance, you welcome the chance to serve the plan.

What does the future hold for 401(k) plans?

As a growing number of baby boomers near retirement age, there is added importance in building wealth for those golden years. There will be more feature-laden programs offered by 401(k) vendors, more potential plan participants and a need for more 401(k) Sales Champions™ to offer value-added support.

Top management at every financial service company that employees financial sales professionals are excited about the future. They understand that as consumers' knowledge of investments grows, their perceived value of an advisor declines. **However, as their assets increase, the value of the guidance of a financial sales professional grows.**

"I think the role of the plan sponsor is going to be examined very carefully during the next decade. I believe the employer will cease to be the gatekeeper. Ultimately, the 401(k) plan will be a retail product where plan sponsors simply send money to wherever they are told (by the plan participants) to send it. Investment advice will be commonplace. Portability will no longer be an issue, since there will be no disruption when a participant changes jobs."
Ted Benna, President, The 401(k) Association.

Source: Institute of Management and Administration (IOMA), 401(k), January 2000

Perhaps one day each American may be able to establish a retirement savings account wherever they want and contribute with direct deposit, regardless of where they work. We will simply provide a smart card to our employer, and the card will be swiped through a computer that instructs the company payroll program where the money is to be deposited and how much money within the maximum limits we can still contribute for the year. You should build relationships with employees who participate in 401(k) plans. If the day comes when plan participants have the option of investing their retirement wealth no matter where they work and anywhere they choose, chances are they will place their accounts with someone they trust. Hopefully, that trusted someone is you, a 401(k) Sales Champion™.

APPENDIX

Table of Contents

Exhibit 1: Employee Survey:
            Local Companies

Exhibit 2: Employee Survey:
           Client Companies

Exhibit 3: Fiduciary Worksheet:
           Annual Review

Exhibit 4: DoL Fee Comparison

Exhibit 5: Written Investment Policy

EXHIBIT
1

Employee Survey:
Local Companies

EMPLOYEE SURVEY: LOCAL COMPANIES
SECTION I

1. RETIREMENT INCOME CAN BE PROVIDED BY THREE SOURCES:
    THE GOVERNMENT, EMPLOYER-SPONSORED RETIREMENT PLANS
    AND AN INDIVIDUAL'S PERSONAL SAVINGS AND INVESTMENTS.
    IN YOUR OPINION, WHO DO YOU THINK HAS THE MAIN
    RESPONSIBILITY FOR PROVIDING RETIREMENT INCOME?

    O THE GOVERNMENT   O THE EMPLOYER
    O INDIVIDUALS THEMSELVES   O DON'T KNOW

2. IN YOUR PARTICULAR SITUATION, WHAT PORTION OF YOUR RETIREMENT
    INCOME DO YOU EXPECT TO COME FROM SOCIAL SECURITY, EMPLOYER
    SPONSORED RETIREMENT PLANS AND YOUR PERSONAL SAVINGS?
    (TOTAL SHOULD EQUAL 100%)

    O FROM GOVERNMENT   %
    O FROM EMPLOYER PLANS   %
    O FROM PERSONAL SAVINGS   %
    O DON'T KNOW   %

3. IF THE GOVERNMENT WERE TO REDUCE THE AMOUNT SPENT ON
    SOCIAL SECURITY AND MEDICARE, HOW WOULD YOU MAKE UP THE
    DIFFERENCE?

    O WORK LONGER AND RETIRE LATER IN LIFE
    O RETIRE AT THE SAME TIME AND TRY TO GET BY WITH LESS
    O INCREASE THE AMOUNT YOU ARE SAVING FOR RETIREMENT
    O OTHER
    O DON'T KNOW

4. DO YOU EXPECT YOUR STANDARD OF LIVING IN RETIREMENT TO BE
    HIGHER, LOWER OR THE SAME AS IN YOUR WORKING YEARS?

    O HIGHER   O LOWER
    O SAME   O DON'T KNOW

5. OVERALL, HOW WELL PREPARED DO YOU THINK YOU ARE FOR
    YOUR EVENTUAL RETIREMENT? WOULD YOU SAY YOU ARE VERY
    WELL PREPARED, SOMEWHAT PREPARED, NOT TOO PREPARED,
    OR NOT AT ALL PREPARED?

    O VERY WELL PREPARED
    O SOMEWHAT PREPARED
    O NOT TOO PREPARED
    O NOT AT ALL PREPARED
    O DON'T KNOW

6. TAKING INTO CONSIDERATION YOUR FINANCIAL SITUATION,
    AT WHAT AGE DO YOU ANTICIPATE BEING ABLE TO AFFORD TO RETIRE?

    O AGE
    O DON'T KNOW

7. HOW WOULD YOU DESCRIBE YOUR PLANS FOR ACHIEVING YOUR
    RETIREMENT SAVINGS GOALS? WOULD YOU SAY YOU HAVE...

    O A COMPREHENSIVE STRATEGY COVERING ALL YOUR GOALS
    O STRATEGIES FOR SOME, BUT NOT ALL OF YOUR GOALS
    O A GENERAL PLAN WITHOUT SPECIFIC STRATEGIES
    O NO DEFINED PLAN OR STRATEGIES
    O DON'T KNOW

8. DO YOU DO MOST OF YOUR FINANCIAL PLANNING ON YOUR OWN,
    WITH THE ASSISTANCE OF A FINANCIAL PROFESSIONAL, OR DO
    YOU NOT DO ANY FINANCIAL PLANNING?

    O DO ON OWN
    O DO WITH THE ASSISTANCE OF A FINANCIAL PROFESSIONAL
    O DON'T DO ANY FINANCIAL PLANNING
    O DON'T KNOW

9. REGARDLESS OF WHETHER OR NOT YOUR EMPLOYER OFFERS THE
    FOLLOWING SERVICES, HOW EFFECTIVE DO YOU FEEL EACH OF THESE
    WOULD BE IN HELPING YOU MAKE INFORMED DECISIONS REGARDING
    YOUR FINANCIAL AND RETIREMENT PLANNING? WOULD THEY BE
    EXTREMELY EFFECTIVE, SOMEWHAT EFFECTIVE, NOT VERY EFFECTIVE
    OR NOT AT ALL EFFECTIVE?

    SEMINARS ON FINANCIAL AND RETIREMENT PLANNING
    O EXTREMELY EFFECTIVE
    O SOMEWHAT EFFECTIVE
    O NOT VERY EFFECTIVE
    O NOT AT ALL EFFECTIVE
    O DON'T KNOW

    **INDIVIDUAL COUNSELING SESSIONS ON FINANCIAL
    AND RETIREMENT PLANNING**
    O EXTREMELY EFFECTIVE
    O SOMEWHAT EFFECTIVE
    O NOT VERY EFFECTIVE
    O NOT AT ALL EFFECTIVE
    O DON'T KNOW

BROCHURES AND NEWSLETTERS ON FINANCIAL AND RETIREMENT PLANNING

○ EXTREMELY EFFECTIVE
○ SOMEWHAT EFFECTIVE
○ NOT VERY EFFECTIVE
○ NOT AT ALL EFFECTIVE
○ DON'T KNOW

VIDEOTAPES OR AUDIOTAPES ON FINANCIAL AND RETIREMENT PLANNING

○ EXTREMELY EFFECTIVE
○ SOMEWHAT EFFECTIVE
○ NOT VERY EFFECTIVE
○ NOT AT ALL EFFECTIVE
○ DON'T KNOW

ON-LINE ACCESS THROUGH YOUR HOME OR OFFICE COMPUTER TO INFORMATION ON FINANCIAL AND RETIREMENT PLANNING

○ EXTREMELY EFFECTIVE
○ SOMEWHAT EFFECTIVE
○ NOT VERY EFFECTIVE
○ NOT AT ALL EFFECTIVE
○ DON'T KNOW

10.   DOES YOUR EMPLOYER PROVIDE A 401(K) PLAN?

○ YES   (GO TO SECTION II)
○ NO   (GO TO SECTION III)
○ DON'T KNOW   (GO TO SECTION III)

SECTION II

1. ARE YOU ELIGIBLE TO PARTICIPATE IN YOUR EMPLOYER'S 401(K) PLAN?

   O YES   GO TO QUESTION 2
   O NO   GO TO QUESTION 3
   O DON'T KNOW   GO TO QUESTION 3

2. DO YOU PARTICIPATE IN YOUR EMPLOYER'S 401(K) PLAN?

   O YES   GO TO QUESTION 4
   O NO   GO TO QUESTION 3

3. IF YOU ARE ELIGIBLE TO PARTICIPATE IN YOUR COMPANY'S 401(K)
   PLAN, BUT CURRENTLY DO NOT, WHAT ARE THE REASONS WHY?
   (PLEASE CHECK ALL THAT APPLY)

   O I CANNOT AFFORD TO SAVE FOR MY RETIREMENT NOW
   O I DO NOT UNDERSTAND HOW THE 401(K) CAN HELP ME
      SAVE FOR MY RETIREMENT
   O I AM NOT CONFIDENT IN HOW TO MANAGE MY 401(K) ACCOUNT
   O OTHER
   O DON'T KNOW

      PLEASE GO TO SECTION III

4. WHAT IS THE MOST IMPORTANT REASON WHY YOU PARTICIPATE
   IN YOUR COMPANY'S 401(K) PLAN?
   (PLEASE CHECK ALL THAT APPLY)

   O SAVE FOR RETIREMENT
   O COMPANY-MATCHING CONTRIBUTIONS
   O TAX-DEFERRED BENEFITS
   O EASE OF SAVING THROUGH PAYROLL DEDUCTION
   O AVAILABILITY OF INVESTMENT CHOICES
   O OTHER
   O DON'T KNOW

5. WHAT PERCENTAGE OF YOUR ANNUAL SALARY DO YOU CONTRIBUTE
   TO YOUR 401(K) PLAN?

   O _____%
   O DON'T KNOW

6. DOES YOUR EMPLOYER MAKE A MATCHING CONTRIBUTION
    TO YOUR ACCOUNT?

    O YES   (GO TO QUESTION 7)
    O NO   (GO TO QUESTION 9)
    O DON'T KNOW   (GO TO QUESTION 9)

7. WHAT PERCENTAGE OF YOUR CONTRIBUTION DOES YOUR EMPLOYER MATCH?

    O _____%
    O DON'T KNOW

8. IF YOUR EMPLOYER DID NOT MATCH YOUR 401(K) CONTRIBUTION,
    WOULD YOU CONTRIBUTE THE SAME AMOUNT THAT YOU DO NOW,
    LESS THAN YOU DO NOW OR MORE THAN YOU DO NOW?

    O SAME AMOUNT THAT YOU DO NOW
    O LESS THAN YOU DO NOW
    O MORE THAN YOU DO NOW
    O DON'T KNOW

9. DOES YOUR EMPLOYER PROVIDE YOU WITH EDUCATIONAL
    MATERIALS TO HELP YOU MAKE YOUR 401(K) PLAN INVESTMENT DECISIONS?

    O YES
    O NO
    O DON'T KNOW

10. HOW USEFUL IS THE INFORMATION IN HELPING YOU MAKE INFORMED
    INVESTMENT DECISIONS? WOULD YOU SAY THE INFORMATION IS VERY
    HELPFUL, SOMEWHAT HELPFUL, NOT VERY HELPFUL OR NOT AT ALL HELPFUL?

    O VERY HELPFUL
    O SOMEWHAT HELPFUL
    O NOT VERY HELPFUL
    O NOT AT ALL HELPFUL
    O DON'T KNOW

11. I WOULD LIKE TO READ A LIST OF STATEMENTS THAT HAVE TO DO
    WITH RETIREMENT PLANNING. FOR EACH, TELL ME IF YOU AGREE
    STRONGLY, AGREE SOMEWHAT, NEITHER AGREE NOR DISAGREE, DISAGREE
    SOMEWHAT OR DISAGREE STRONGLY.

**I AM CONCERNED ABOUT OUTLIVING THE MONEY
THAT I WILL PUT AWAY FOR RETIREMENT**

- ○ AGREE STRONGLY
- ○ AGREE SOMEWHAT
- ○ NEITHER AGREE NOR DISAGREE
- ○ DISAGREE SOMEWHAT
- ○ DISAGREE STRONGLY
- ○ DON'T KNOW

I KNOW THAT I COULD SAVE MORE THAN I DO NOW

- ○ AGREE STRONGLY
- ○ AGREE SOMEWHAT
- ○ NEITHER AGREE NOR DISAGREE
- ○ DISAGREE SOMEWHAT
- ○ DISAGREE STRONGLY
- ○ DON'T KNOW

**THE BEST WAY FOR ME TO SAVE IS TO HAVE MY MONEY
AUTOMATICALLY DEDUCTED ON A REGULAR BASIS FROM MY PAYCHECK**

- ○ AGREE STRONGLY
- ○ AGREE SOMEWHAT
- ○ NEITHER AGREE NOR DISAGREE
- ○ DISAGREE SOMEWHAT
- ○ DISAGREE STRONGLY
- ○ DON'T KNOW

**BY USING TAX-DEFERRED ACCOUNTS LIKE A 401(K) PLAN,
MY SAVINGS WILL GROW MUCH FASTER THAN WITH A REGULAR
TAXABLE SAVINGS ACCOUNT**

- ○ AGREE STRONGLY
- ○ AGREE SOMEWHAT
- ○ NEITHER AGREE NOR DISAGREE
- ○ DISAGREE SOMEWHAT
- ○ DISAGREE STRONGLY
- ○ DON'T KNOW

I SHOULD HAVE STARTED SAVING FOR RETIREMENT MUCH SOONER

- ○ AGREE STRONGLY
- ○ AGREE SOMEWHAT
- ○ NEITHER AGREE NOR DISAGREE
- ○ DISAGREE SOMEWHAT
- ○ DISAGREE STRONGLY
- ○ DON'T KNOW

12.   THERE ARE SEVERAL WAYS THAT YOUR COMPANY CAN ENHANCE
       YOUR 401(K) PLAN. WHICH OF THE FOLLOWING ENHANCEMENTS
       WOULD BE MOST BENEFICIAL TO YOU?
       (PLEASE CHECK ALL THAT APPLY)

   O   MORE FREQUENT STATEMENTS
   O   MORE TIMELY STATEMENTS
   O   MORE INVESTMENT CHOICES
   O   BETTER PERFORMING INVESTMENT CHOICES
   O   ON-SITE REGULARLY SCHEDULED RETIREMENT SEMINARS
   O   HARD COPY MATERIALS SUCH AS NEWSLETTERS AND BROCHURES
   O   800# ACCESS TO YOUR ACCOUNT
   O   ON-LINE ACCESS TO YOUR ACCOUNT
   O   COACHING FROM A FINANCIAL SALES PROFESSIONAL

       PLEASE GO TO SECTION III

SECTION III

1.   SEX

    ○ MALE   ○ FEMALE

2.   WHAT IS YOUR AGE?

    ○ LESS THAN 25 YEARS
    ○ 25 TO 44 YEARS
    ○ 45 TO 64 YEARS
    ○ 65 OR OLDER

3.   WHAT IS YOUR MARTIAL STATUS?

    ○ SINGLE
    ○ MARRIED
    ○ DIVORCED
    ○ WIDOWED

4.   WHAT IS YOUR TOTAL HOUSEHOLD INCOME BEFORE TAXES?

    ○ UNDER $30,000
    ○ $30,000 TO UNDER $40,000
    ○ $40,000 TO UNDER $50,000
    ○ $50,000 TO UNDER $75,000
    ○ $75,000 TO UNDER $100,000
    ○ OVER $100,000

5.   WHAT IS THE SIZE OF YOUR SAVINGS AND INVESTMENT PORTFOLIO, INCLUDING ALL SOURCES?

    ○ UNDER $10,000
    ○ $10,000 TO UNDER $25,000
    ○ $25,000 TO UNDER $50,000
    ○ $50,000 TO UNDER $100,000
    ○ $100,000 TO UNDER $250,000
    ○ $250,000 TO UNDER $500,000
    ○ $500,000 TO UNDER $1,000,000
    ○ OVER $1,000,000

NAME _____

ADDRESS _____

PHONE _____ EMPLOYER _____

THANK YOU VERY MUCH FOR TAKING THE TIME TO COMPLETE THIS SURVEY.
WE WILL MAIL RESULTS TO YOU AT THE COMPLETION OF THE SURVEY.

APPENDIX

EXHIBIT 2

Employee Survey:
Client Companies

EMPLOYEE SURVEY: CLIENT COMPANIES

AS AN EMPLOYEE OF COMPANY NAME, YOU HAVE THE ABILITY TO SAVE YOUR MONEY FOR YOUR RETIREMENT YEARS THROUGH COMPANY NAME SAVINGS PLAN. COMPANY NAME WANTS TO ENSURE THAT YOUR SAVINGS PLAN CAN HELP YOU TO ACCOMPLISH YOUR RETIREMENT SAVINGS GOAL BY OFFERING YOU AN OPTIMAL RETIREMENT SAVINGS PROGRAM.

THE PURPOSE OF THIS SURVEY IS TO GAUGE YOUR LEVEL OF SATISFACTION WITH YOUR COMPANY SAVINGS PLAN, AND HOW WELL YOU BELIEVE THAT THE SAVINGS PLAN IS HELPING YOU TO REALIZE YOUR RETIREMENT SAVINGS GOAL. PLEASE COMPLETE THE SURVEY AND RETURN IT TO _____ BY _____. PLEASE DO NOT PUT YOUR NAME ON THE SURVEY UNLESS YOU WISH TO. THANK YOU FOR YOUR INSIGHTS, THEY WILL HELP COMPANY NAME TO MAINTAIN AN OPTIMAL RETIREMENT SAVINGS PLAN FOR YOU.

1.   ARE YOU CURRENTLY ELIGIBLE TO JOIN THE COMPANY SAVINGS PLAN?

    O YES   O NO

2.   DO YOU CURRENTLY PARTICIPATE IN THE COMPANY SAVINGS PLAN?

    O YES   O NO

    (IF YOU ANSWER NO TO QUESTIONS #1 AND #2, PLEASE COMPLETE QUESTION #3, AND QUESTION #4, THEN TURN IN YOUR SURVEY, THANK YOU.)

3.   IF YOU ARE ELIGIBLE TO JOIN AND PARTICIPATE IN THE COMPANY SAVINGS PLAN, BUT CURRENTLY DO NOT, WHAT ARE THE REASONS WHY? PLEASE RANK YOUR RESPONSES FROM 1 TO 5, WITH 1 BEING YOUR MOST IMPORTANT REASON WHY AND 5 BEING THE LEAST IMPORTANT REASON YOU DO NOT PARTICIPATE IN THE ABC COMPANY401(K) SAVINGS PLAN.

    __I CANNOT AFFORD TO SAVE FOR MY RETIREMENT NOW.
    __I DO NOT UNDERSTAND HOW COMPANY NAME
      SAVINGS PLAN CAN HELP ME TO SAVE FOR MY RETIREMENT YEARS.
    __I AM NOT CONFIDENT ON HOW TO MANAGE MY SAVINGS ACCOUNT.
    __I AM NOT CONFIDENT IN THE FINANCIAL INSTITUTION THAT HOLDS
      AND INVESTS MY MONEY.
    __I HAVE NOT RECEIVED ENOUGH INFORMATION FROM COMPANY NAME
      TO HELP ME TO UNDERSTAND THE SAVINGS PLAN.

4. THE LIST BELOW SHOWS SEVERAL WAYS THAT CAN ENHANCE THE
    CORPORATION SAVINGS PLAN. PLEASE RANK THE METHODS IN THE
    ORDER YOU BELIEVE WOULD BE MOST BENEFICIAL TO YOU, WITH
    1 BEING THE MOST BENEFICIAL AND 8 BEING THE LEAST BENEFICIAL
    IMPROVEMENT FOR YOU.

    __MORE FREQUENT STATEMENTS
    __MORE TIMELY STATEMENTS
    __MORE INVESTMENT CHOICES
    __BETTER PERFORMING INVESTMENT RETURN CHOICES
    __ON-SITE RETIREMENT/ INVESTMENT EDUCATION SEMINARS,
       REGULARLY SCHEDULED
    __HARDCOPY, SUCH AS NEWSLETTERS AND BROCHURES COVERING
       TOPICS SUCH AS RETIREMENT PLANNING AND INVESTMENT
       MANAGEMENT
    __AN "800" NUMBER WHICH YOU CAN CALL 24 HOURS A DAY, AND GET
       INFORMATION ON YOUR ACCOUNT
    __EASY TO UNDERSTAND INFORMATION ON WHAT A 401(K) PLAN IS,
       AND HOW THE 401(K) PLAN CAN HELP ME TO ACCOMPLISH MY
       RETIREMENT SAVINGS GOAL

5. PLEASE RANK THE MOST IMPORTANT REASONS WHY YOU PARTICIPATE IN
    THE COMPANY SAVINGS PLAN, WITH 1 BEING THE MOST IMPORTANT AND 5
    THE LEAST IMPORTANT REASON.

    __SAVE FOR RETIREMENT
    __CORPORATION CONTRIBUTIONS
    __TAX-DEFERRED BENEFITS
    __EASE OF SAVING THROUGH PAYROLL DEDUCTION
    __AVAILABLE INVESTMENT CHOICES

6. HOW CONFIDENT ARE YOU IN SELECTING AMONGST THE INVESTMENT
    CHOICES OFFERED THROUGH THE COMPANY SAVINGS PLAN?

    __EXTREMELY CONFIDENT
    __SOMEWHAT CONFIDENT
    __ NOT TOO CONFIDENT
    __ NOT AT ALL CONFIDENT

7.   THE LIST BELOW SHOWS SEVERAL WAYS THAT RETIREMENT PLANNING AND INVESTMENT INFORMATION COULD BE DELIVERED TO YOU. PLEASE RANK THE METHODS IN THE ORDER YOU BELIEVE WOULD BE MOST BENEFICIAL TO YOU, WITH 1 BEING THE MOST BENEFICIAL AND 3 BEING THE LEAST BENEFICIAL.

___PERSONAL MEETING WITH A FINANCIAL PROFESSIONAL TO HELP ME SET MY RETIREMENT SAVINGS GOAL, TO IMPLEMENT MY RETIREMENT SAVINGS PLAN AND TO BETTER UNDERSTAND THE OBJECTIVES I NEED TO COMPLETE IN ORDER TO ACCOMPLISH MY RETIREMENT SAVINGS GOAL

___ON-SITE RETIREMENT AND INVESTMENT EDUCATION SEMINARS

___BETTER, MORE INFORMATIVE MATERIALS, SUCH AS A NEWSLETTER, FLIERS, AND BROCHURES COVERING TOPICS OF RETIREMENT AND INVESTMENT EDUCATION.

8.   IF INVESTMENT CHOICES WERE ADDED, THAT OFFERED THE CHANCE TO ACHIEVE GREATER INVESTMENT RETURN IN EXCHANGE FOR GREATER RISK, HOW LIKELY WOULD YOU BE IN INVESTING AMONG THOSE CHOICES?

___VERY LIKELY

___SOMEWHAT LIKELY

___NOT TOO LIKELY

___NOT AT ALL LIKELY

9.   HOW MANY INVESTMENT CHOICES DO YOU HAVE TO INVEST YOUR MONEY AMONG IN THE COMPANY SAVINGS PLAN?

___ONE

___TWO

___THREE

___FOUR

___FIVE

___MORE THAN SIX

10.   HOW MANY OF THE CURRENT INVESTMENT CHOICES, DO YOU INVEST YOUR MONEY AMONG?

___ONE

___TWO

___THREE

___FOUR

___FIVE

___SIX

___MORE THAN SIX

11. HOW WOULD YOU DESCRIBE YOURSELF WHEN IT COMES TO YOUR
    INVESTMENT MANAGEMENT STYLE?

    ___CONSERVATIVE
    ___MODERATE
    ___AGGRESSIVE
    ___VERY AGGRESSIVE

12. PLEASE WRITE IN THE AREA BELOW ANY COMMENTS THAT YOU HAVE TO
    IMPROVE THE COMPANY SAVINGS PLAN.

    _____
    _____
    _____
    _____
    _____
    _____
    _____
    _____
    _____
    _____

    PLEASE RETURN YOUR COMPLETED SURVEY TO _____, BY _____.
    THANK YOU FOR YOUR INSIGHTS AND PARTICIPATION.

EXHIBIT

3

Fiduciary Worksheet: Annual Review

Introduction

This worksheet has been designed to help 401(k) plan sponsors to identify issues, suggest enhancements and monitor plan investments and employee retirement education programs.

You should retain this worksheet with all other investment management and employee retirement education materials in your files as documentation attesting to management of fiduciary duties.

Name of Plan:_____

Individuals involved with the 401(k) plan evaluation on _____20___

Name:_____ Title:_____
Name:_____ Title:_____
Name:_____ Title:_____
Name:_____ Title:_____
Name:_____ Title:_____
Name:_____ Title:_____
Name:_____ Title:_____
Name:_____ Title:_____

Date of previous evaluation:_____

Plan information as of evaluation date:

Number of eligible employees:_____

Number of participating employees:_____

Percent participation:_____

Previous evaluation percent participation:___

Describe general events which impacted the 401(k) plan during this evaluation period.

_____

_____

Name of Plan Investments:	Type of investment:

Option #1:_____
Option #2:_____
Option #3:_____
Option #4:_____
Option #5:_____
Option #6:_____
Option #7:_____
Option #8:_____
Option #9:_____
Option #10:_____

Plan Asset Analysis as of:_____ 200__
Previous Plan Asset Analysis:____ 200__

Investment Option:	Value of the Assets in The investment:	Pct. (%) of total Plan Assets	Previous Pct. (%) of total Plan Assets

(1) _____
(2) _____
(3) _____
(4) _____
(5) _____
(6) _____
(7) _____
(8) _____
(9) _____
(10) _____

Investment Policy Investment Matrix Reviewed: ____Yes ____No

Describe events which impacted the plan assets during this evaluation period (if any).

_____
_____
_____
_____
_____

Employee Retirement Education Events:

Date:_____
Outline:_____YES _____NO
Sign-up sheets:_____YES _____NO
Copies of materials distributed to employees: _____YES _____NO
Plan Sponsor Book entry:_____YES _____NO

Date:_____
Outline:_____YES _____NO
Sign-up sheets:_____YES _____NO
Copies of materials distributed to employees: _____YES _____NO
Plan Sponsor Book entry:_____YES _____NO

Date:_____
Outline:_____YES _____NO
Sign-up sheets:_____YES _____NO
Copies of materials distributed to employees: _____YES _____NO
Plan Sponsor Book entry:_____YES _____NO

Date:_____
Outline:_____YES _____NO
Sign-up sheets:_____YES _____NO
Copies of materials distributed to employees: _____YES _____NO
Plan Sponsor Book entry:_____YES _____NO

Employees' survey results as of:_____200__

Initiatives for the 401(k) plan:

○ 1

○ 2

○ 3

○ 4

○ 5

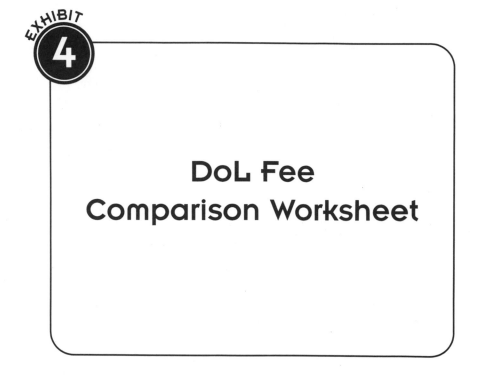

EXHIBIT

4

DoL Fee
Comparison Worksheet

ABC Company
401(k) PLAN FEE DISCLOSURE FORM

Contact Name:_____

Institution:_____

Phone:_____

I. Investment product fees (See Schedule A)   Amount/ Estimate

    A. Collective Investment Fund(s) $_____
    B. Insurance/ Annuity Product(s) $_____
    C. Mutual Fund(s) $_____
    D. Individually Managed Account(s) $_____
    E. Brokerage Window $_____
    F. Other Product(s) (Specify) $_____
       Total Investment Products Fees $_____

II. Plan Administration Expense (See Schedule B)
    Total Plan Administration Expenses $_____
III. Plan Start-Up or Conversion Related charges (See Schedule C)
    One Time Start-up / Conversion Expenses $_____
IV. Service Provider Termination-Related charges (See Schedule D)
    Service Provider termination expenses $_____

    Total Plan expenses $_____

For definitions of terms throughout this disclosure form, see Schedule E.

Amounts are calculated based on rates charged, which are identified in attached schedules as applied to relevant information (for example amount of assets or number of participants). Certain calculations may be estimates based on information provided by the plan sponsor, and may vary as circumstances change.

ABC Company
401(k) PLAN FEE DISCLOSURE FORM

Schedule A
Investment Product Fees/Estimates

Collective Investment Fund	Assets as of / /	Management Fees	Other (specify)	Total Cost
Fund 1				
Fund 2				
Fund 3				
Fund 4				
Fund 5				
Fund 6				
Fund 7				
Fund 8				
Fund 9				
Fund 10				
Fund 11				
Fund 12				
TOTAL				

ABC Company
401(k) PLAN FEE DISCLOSURE FORM

Schedule A, continued
Investment Product Fees/Estimates

TOTAL Insurance/Annuity Product	Assest as of / /	Mangement Fees	Mortality Risk and Administrative Expense (M&E)	Other (Specify)	TOTAL COST
Fund 1					
Fund 2					
Fund 3					
Fund 4					
Fund 5					
Fund 6					
Fund 7					
Fund 8					
Fund 9					
Fund 10					
Separate Account 1					
Separate Account 2					
Separate Account 3					
Separate Account 4					
Separate Account 5					
Separate Account 6					
Separate Account 7					
Separate Account 8					
Separate Account 9					
Separate Account 10					
TOTAL					

ABC Company
401(k) PLAN FEE DISCLOSURE FORM

Schedule A continued
Investment Product Fees/Estimates

Mutual Fund	Assest as of / /	Expense Ratio including 12b-1 and management fee	Front-end Load	Other (Specify)	TOTAL COST
Fund 1					
Fund 2					
Fund 3					
Fund 4					
Fund 5					
Fund 6					
Fund 7					
Fund 8					
Fund 9					
Fund 10					
Fund 11					
Fund 12					
TOTAL					

ABC Company
401(k) PLAN FEE DISCLOSURE FORM

Schedule A continued
Investment Product Fees/Estimates

Individually Managed Account	Assest as of / /	Management Fees	Other (Specify)	TOTAL COST
Project 1				
Project 2				
Project 3				
Project 4				
Project 5				
Project 6				
Project 7				
Project 8				
Project 9				
Project 10				
Project 11				
Project 12				
TOTAL				

ABC Company
401(k) PLAN FEE DISCLOSURE FORM
Schedule A continued
Investment Product Fees/Estimates

Brokerage Window Fund	Assets as of / /	Commission (range)	Transaction Fee (range)	Other (specify)	Total Cost
Total Transactions					

Other Fund	Assets as of / /	Management Fees	Other (specify)	Total Cost
Product 1				
Product 2				
Product 3				
Product 4				
Product 5				
Product 6				
Product 7				
Product 8				
Product 9				
Product 10				
Product 11				
Product 12				
Total				

Total Investment Product Fees $ _____

Schedule A continued
Investment Product Fees/Estimates

Fees represent product-related charges paid by the plan. Fees associated with the participants' transfer of account balances between investment options, including investment transfer expenses and any contingent back-end loads, redemption fees and surrender charges should be included in "other" expenses. In addition, any wrap fees or pricing charges for non-publicly traded assets should be included in the "other" expenses column. For investment product termination fees associated with the plan termination or conversion, see Schedule D. Insurance companies incur marketing and distribution costs, which are recouped through charges assessed against the plan.

Includes 12b-1 fee and management fee. (See the fee table in the fund prospectus.)

Fees associated with the participants' transfer of account balances between investment options, including investment transfer expenses and any contingent back-end loads, redemption fees and surrender charges should be included in "other" expenses. In addition, any wrap fees or pricing charges for non-publicly traded assets should be included in the "other" expenses column. For investment product termination fees associated with plan termination or conversion, see schedule D. Insurance companies incur marketing and distribution costs, which are recouped through charges assessed against the plan.

Other products could include investment vehicles such as REITs and limited partnerships.

ABC Company
401(k) PLAN FEE DISCLOSURE FORM

Schedule B
Plan Administration Expenses

Expense Type	Rate Estimate	Bundled Service Arrangement Please ✓	Total Cost
Administration / Recordkeeping Fees:			
Daily Valuation	$_____	_____	$_____
Payroll Processing	$_____	_____	$_____
Balance Inquiry	$_____	_____	$_____
Investment Transfer	$_____	_____	$_____
Contract Administration Charge	$_____	_____	$_____
Distribution Processing	$_____	_____	$_____
QDRO Processing	$_____	_____	$_____
Participant Statements	$_____	_____	$_____
Plan Sponsor Reports	$_____	_____	$_____
VRU / Internet Services	$_____	_____	$_____
Other (specify)	$_____	_____	$_____
Subtotal:			$_____
Participation Education / Advice:	$_____	_____	$_____
Participant Education	$_____	_____	$_____
Materials / Distribution	$_____	_____	$_____
Education Meetings (frequency)	$_____	_____	$_____
Investment Advice Programs	$_____	_____	$_____
Other (specify)	$_____	_____	$_____
Subtotal:			$_____
Trustee / Custodial Services:	$_____	_____	$_____
Certified Annual Trust Statement	$_____	_____	$_____
Safekeeping of Plan Assets	$_____	_____	$_____
Other (specify)	$_____	_____	$_____
Subtotal:			$_____

Amount represents the method by which the fee is calculated, for example as a percentage of plan assets under management, based upon number of participants or based upon number of transactions. For start-up or take-over situations, fees are based upon estimates and /or certain assumptions, i.e., regarding assets under management and number of participants. Services provided under a bundled services arrangement are indicated by a check mark next to a specific service. Amount represents flat dollar amount charges based upon the particular method of calculation. In some instances, these amounts represent estimates based on assumptions provided by the plan sponsor.

ABC Company
401(k) PLAN FEE DISCLOSURE FORM

Schedule B
Plan Administration Expenses

Expense Type	Rate Estimate	Bundled Service Arrangement Please ✓	Total Cost
Compliance Services:			
Nondiscrimination Testing	$_____	_____	$_____
Signature Ready Form 5500	$_____	_____	$_____
Annual Audit	$_____	_____	$_____
Other (specify)	$_____	_____	$_____
Subtotal:			$_____
Plan Amendment Fee:			
Plan Amendment Fee	$_____	_____	$_____
Plan Document Design	$_____	_____	$_____
Letter of Determination	$_____	_____	$_____
Preperation Fee	$_____	_____	$_____
Other (specify)	$_____	_____	$_____
Subtotal:			$_____
Loan Adminstration:			
Loan Origination	$_____	_____	$_____
Loan Processig Fee	$_____	_____	$_____
Loan Maintenance and			
Repayment Tracking Fee	$_____	_____	$_____
Other (specify)	$_____	_____	$_____
Subtotal:			$_____
Total Separate Charges			$_____
Total Bundled Services			$_____
(Less Offsets/Credits Paid to the Plan)			$(_____)
Total Plan Administration Expenses			$_____

Amount represents the method by which the fee is calculated, for example as a percentage of plan assets under management, based upon number of participants or based upon number of transactions. For start-up or take-over situations, fees are based upon estimates and /or certain assumptions, i.e., regarding assets under management and number of participants. Services provided under a bundled services arrangement are indicated by a check mark next to a specific service. Amount represents flat dollar amount charges based upon the particular method of calculation. In some instances, these amounts represent estimates based on assumptions provided by the plan sponsor.

ABC Company
401(k) PLAN FEE DISCLOSURE FORM

Schedule C
One-Time Start-Up / Conversion Expenses

Expense Type	Rate Estimate	Total Cost
Start-up / Conversion Education Program	$_____	$_____
Start-up / Conversion Enrollment Expense	$_____	$_____
Installation Fee	$_____	$_____
Start-up / Conversion Plan Document Fee	$_____	$_____
Filing Fee	$_____	$_____
Other (specify)	$_____	$_____

Total Start-up / Conversion Expenses

Amount represents the method by which the fee is calculated, for example as a percentage of plan assets under management, based upon number of participants or based upon number of transactions. For start-up or take-over situations, fees are based upon estimates and /or certain assumptions, i.e., regarding assets under management and number of participants. Services provided under a bundled services arrangement are indicated by a check mark next to a specific service. Amount represents flat dollar amount charges based upon the particular method of calculation. In some instances, these amounts represent estimates based on assumptions provided by the plan sponsor.

ABC Company
401(k) PLAN FEE DISCLOSURE FORM

Schedule D
Service Provider Termination Expenses

Expense Type	Rate Estimate	Total Cost
Investment Product Expenses		
Contract Termination Charges	$_____	$_____
Back-end Loan	$_____	$_____
Product Termination Fee	$_____	$_____
Other (Specify)	$_____	$_____
Total		$_____
Plan Administrative Expenses		
Service Provider Termination Charge	$_____	$_____
Service Contract Termination Charge	$_____	$_____
Other (Specify)	$_____	$_____
Total Termination Expenses		$_____

Amount represents the method by which the fee is calculated, for example as a percentage of plan assets under management, based upon number of participants or based upon number of transactions. For start-up or take-over situations, fees are based upon estimates and /or certain assumptions, i.e., regarding assets under management and number of participants. Services provided under a bundled services arrangement are indicated by a check mark next to a specific service. Amount represents flat dollar amount charges based upon the particular method of calculation. In some instances, these amounts represent estimates based on assumptions provided by the plan sponsor.

ABC Company
401(k) PLAN FEE DISCLOSURE FORM

Schedule E
Definition of Terms

Administrative/Recordkeeping Fee: Fee for providing recordkeeping and other plan participant administrative services. For start-up or takeover plans, these fees typically include charges for contacting and processing information from the prior service provider and "matching up" or mapping participant information. Use of this term is not meant to identify any ERISA Section 3(16)(A) obligations.

Annual Audit: Federal law requires that all ERISA-covered plans with more than 100 participants be audited by an independent auditor. It is also common to refer to a DoI or IRS examination of a plan as a plan audit. Any charge imposed by a service provider in connection with this audit is reflected on schedule B.

Back-end Load: Sales charges due upon the sale or transfer of mutual funds, insurance/ annuity products or other investments, which may be reduced and/or eliminated over time.

Balance Inquiry: Fee that may be charged each time a participant inquires about his or her balance.

Brokerage Commission: A fee paid to a broker or other intermediary for executing a trade.

Brokerage Window: A plan investment option allowing a participant to establish a self-directed brokerage account.

Bundled Services: Arrangements whereby plan service providers offer 401(k) plan establishment, investment services and administration for an all-inclusive fee. Bundled services by their nature and cannot be priced on a per service basis.

Collective Investment Fund: A tax-exempt pooled fund operated by a bank or trust company that commingles the assets of trust accounts for which the bank provides fiduciary services.

Contract Administration Charge: An omnibus charge for costs of administering the insurance/annuity contract, including costs associated with the maintenance of participant accounts and all investment-related transactions initiated by participants.

Contract Termination Charge: A charge to the plan for "surrendering" or "terminating" its insurance/annuity contract prior to the end of a stated time period. The charge typically decreases over time.

Conversion: The process of changing from one service provider to another.

Distribution Expense: The cost typically associated with processing paperwork and issuing a check for a distribution of plan assets to a participant. May include the generation of IRS Form 1099R. This fee may apply to hardship and other in-service withdrawals as well as to separation-from service or retirement distributions.

Eligible Employee: Any employee who is eligible to participate in and receive benefits from a plan.

Expense Ratio: The cost of investing and administering assets, including management fees, in a mutual fund or other collective fund expressed as a percentage of total assets.

Front-end Load: Sales charge incurred when an investment in a mutual fund is made.

Individually Managed Account: An investment account managed for a single plan.

Installation Fee: One-time fee for initiating new services.

Investment Transfer Expense: Fee associated with a participant changing his or her investment allocation, or making transfers among funding accounts under the plan.

Loan Maintenance and Repayment Tracking Fee: Fee charged to monitor outstanding loans and repayment schedule.

Loan Origination Fee: Fee charged when a plan loan is originally taken.

Loan Processing Fee: Fee charged to process a plan loan application.

Management Fee: Fee charged for the management of pooled investments such as collective investments, mutual funds and individually managed accounts.

Mortality Risk and Administrative Expense (M&E Fee): Fee charged by an insurance company to cover the cost of the insurance features of an annuity contract, including the guarantee of a lifetime income payment, interest and expense guarantees, and any death benefit provided during the accumulation period.

Nondiscrimination Testing Expense: Tax-qualified retirement plans must be administered in compliance with several regulations requiring numerical measurements. The fee charged for the process of determining whether the plan is in compliance is collectively called nondiscrimination testing expense.

Participant: Person who has an account in the plan.

Participant Education Materials/Distribution Expenses: All costs (including travel expenses) associated with providing print, video, software and /or live instruction to educate employees about how the plan works, the plan investment funds, and asset allocation strategies. There may be a one-time cost associated with implementing a new plan, as well as ongoing costs for an existing program.

Plan Document/Determination Letter Fee (Filing Fee): Fee charged for a written plan document. Fee can also include the costs associated with preparing and filing IRS-required documentation, including the request for a determination letter (document issued by the IRS stating whether the plan meets the qualifications for tax-advantaged treatment).

Plan Loan: The law allows participants to borrow from their accounts up to prescribed limits. This is an optional plan feature.

Product Termination Fee: Investment-product charges associated with terminating one or all of a service provider's investment products.

QDRO (Qualified Domestic Relations Order): A judgment, decree or order that creates or recognizes an alternate payee's (such as former spouse, child, etc.) right to receive all or a portion of a participant's retirement plan benefits.

Separate Account: An asset account established by a life insurance company, separate from other funds of the life insurance company, offering investment funding options for pension plans.

Service Provider Termination Charge: Plan administrative costs associated with terminating a relationship with a service provider, with the permanent termination of a plan, or with the termination of specific plan services. These may be termed "surrender" or "transfer" charges.

Signature Ready Form 5500: Fee to prepare Form 5500, a form which all qualified retirement plans (excluding SEPs and Simple IRAs) must file annually with the IRS.

Start-up/Enrollment Expense: Costs associated with providing materials to educate employees about the plan, and enrolling employees in the plan. This may be part of, or included in, the education programs. There may be a one-time cost associated with implementing a new plan, as well as ongoing enrollment costs.

Trustee Services: Fees charged by the individual, bank or trust company with fiduciary responsibility for holding plan assets.

VRU: Voice Response Unit.

Wrap Fee: An inclusive fee generally based on the percentage of assets in an investment program, which typically provides asset allocation, execution of transactions and other administrative services.

12b-1 Fee: A charge to shareholders to cover a mutual fund's shareholder servicing, distribution and marketing costs.

EXHIBIT
5

Written Investment Policy

Please have your office Compliance Officer review any outgoing correspondance before sending.

WRITTEN INVESTMENT POLICY STATEMENT
ABC Company, Inc.
PURPOSE

The purpose of this Written Investment Policy Statement is to establish a clear understanding between the Investment Committee and the ABC Company, Inc. 401(k) plan participants of the ABC Company, Inc. 401(k) plan investment choices. This Written Investment Policy Statement will outline an overall philosophy that is specific enough for the ABC Company, Inc. 401(k) plan participants to know what is expected of each investment choice, thus aiding in their investment decisions. Through this Written Investment Policy Statement, the Investment Committee will provide realistic risk policies to serve as standards for the evaluation of each investment choice, ongoing investment performance, as well as outline procedures for the acquisition, holding, and disposing of investment choices. This Written Investment Policy Statement will be reviewed annually by the Investment Committee.

BACKGROUND

The ABC Company, Inc. 401(k) plan was started in 200X and is the primary employee retirement program sponsored by ABC Company, Inc.. The Investment Committee will select the investment menu for the ABC Company, Inc. 401(k) plan with the long-term interests of the plan participants and their beneficiaries in mind.

As of December 31, 200X, XXX employees were eligible to participate in the ABC Company, Inc. 401(k) plan. XXX employees actively salary defer and receive an employer match of $0.xx for every dollar up to x% of their salary deferral. A discretionary profit sharing contribution of x% was made for all eligible employees in 200X.

KEY INFORMATION

Name of Plan:	ABC Company, Inc. 401(k) Plan
Plan Sponsor:	ABC Company, Inc.
Plan IRS Identification:	12345678
Investment Committee Members:	Member A
	Member B
	Member C
	Member D

Custodian:	XYZ Investment Firm
Plan Administrator:	ABC Company, Inc.
Investment Choices:	A) Stable Principal
	B) Domestic Growth and Income
	C) Domestic Growth
	D) International Growth

INVESTMENT OBJECTIVES

Investment choices of the ABC Company,Inc 401(k) Plan will be chosen and annually evaluated for the purpose of providing benefits to the plan participants. The Investment Committee has established four broad investment categories for the participants to allocate their account balances. The four categories include:

- Stable Principal
- Domestic Growth and Income
- Domestic Growth
- International Growth

Below is a discussion of each respective investment choice's portfolio composition objectives as well as the benchmark to which its performance will be assessed against.
Recognizing that short-term market fluctuation may cause variations in each investment choice's performance, the Investment Committee will evaluate each investment choice's performance over a three-year period.

- Stable Principal: The portfolio will invest in investment-grade instruments which will provide a stable $1.00 net asset value per unit pricing. The yield of this investment choice can fluctuate daily, yet the net asset value of $1.00 per unit will never vary. The investment choice should return on an annual basis the XXX Money Market Fund Index.

- Domestic/Global Growth and Income: The portfolio will invest at the discretion of the portfolio manager in stocks, bonds, and cash. The percent invested in each should comply with the following guidelines:
  - A) Cash: 0% to 5%
  - B) Bonds: 20% to 80%
  - C) Stocks: 20% to 80%

The Growth and Income investment choice should approximate the XXX Growth and Income Funds Index.

- Domestic Growth: The portfolio will invest primarily in stocks, and at the discretion of the portfolio manager, may hold a certain portion of the portfolio in cash for defensive purposes. The Growth investment option should approximate the XXXXXX Growth Funds Index.

- International Growth: The portfolio will invest primarily in stocks, and at the discretion of the portfolio manager, may hold a certain portion of the portfolio in cash for defensive purposes. The International Growth investment choice should approximate the XXX International Funds Index.

ACQUISITION-HOLDING-DISPOSITION OF INVESTMENT CHOICES

The decision by the Investment Committee to acquire, hold or dispose of an investment choice will be accomplished after an extensive review of the benefits (or lack of) that the investment choice affords to the ABC Company, Inc. 401(k) plan participants.

Any additional investment choice will be analyzed by comparing against its respective benchmark, year-to-date, three-year, and inception-to-date net performance. Total expense ratios will be taken into consideration, as will the candidate investment choice beta. Longevity of the existing portfolio manager will weigh positively in the decision to acquire the candidate investment choice.

Any existing investment choice will be reviewed annually by the Investment Committee to determine to continue to hold the investment choice or to dispose of the investment choice.

Disposition of an existing investment choice will be accomplished after an extensive review by the Investment Committee. Issues that can cause the Investment Committee to dispose of an existing investment choice include:

- 100 basis point under performance versus the respective benchmark over a tw0- year period of time.

- An increase of over 50 basis points in the investment choice expense ratio.

- A radical change in the asset class and/or individual securities in which the investment manager can invest.

- The current investment manager relinquishing responsibility for management of the investment choice.

- Any circumstances which the members of the Investment Committee believe are substantial enough to warrant review of the investment choice.

INVESTMENT COMMITTEE SIGN-OFF

This Written Investment Policy Statement will be reviewed annually by the Investment Committee to accomplish its goal in providing benefit for the participants of the ABC Company, Inc. 401(k) plan. The Investment Committee welcomes any participant to comment on this Written Investment Policy Statement and /or any investment choice.

Signed:

_____   _____
Investment Committee Member   Investment Committee Member

_____   _____
Investment Committee Member   Investment Committee Member

Disclaimer

The purpose of this book is to provide a general resource guide and reference manual for the financial sales professional. Neither the authors, KnowHow 401(k) LLC, their affiliates, subsidiaries or agents make any express or implied warranties regarding the information supplied herein. Anyone who decides to acquire 401(k) plans must invest a lot of time and effort as this is not a "get-rich-quick" scheme.

Actionable Ideas Index

Marketplace Facts Page

1. More employees participate in DC plans than DB plans — 2
2. Top 10 401(k) program vendors — 3
3. Future growth of the 401(k) market — 9
4. Majority of eligible employees participate in their company 401(k) plan — 10
5. 401(k) participation and marketplace asset statistics — 10
6. Ranking per financial sales professional of participant investment advice — 15
7. Why small-business employers sponsor 401(k) plans — 20
8. Current DoL regulations on the timeliness of employer deposits of employee 401(k) contributions — 24
9. 401(k) plan asset allocation by financial service company — 26
10. ERISA: employer duties — 27
11. ERISA: Title 1 — 28
12. Unemployment rate in the 1990s — 32
13. Raising the contribution limit for 401(k) plans by individuals — 33
14. Company-matching contributions — 48
15. Cost of Plan Sponsorship — 49
16. Plan participants pay for more recordkeeping fees — 50
17. Pension Welfare Benefits Administration Study of 401(k) Plan Fees and Expenses — 51
18. Mutual fund fees are declining — 52
19. Social Security Administration free personal earnings and benefits estimate — 53
20. ERISA: prudent expert — 54
21. The federal agencies which govern private pension plans — 55
22. Complying with regulation 404(c) — 55
23. Business plan writing assistance — 61
24. Plan participants alter their behaviors with technology advancements — 70
25. Top three reasons plan sponsors change 401(k) vendors — 71
26. Mean number of investment choices in 401(k) plans — 106
27. Black-out period just got shorter — 130
28. Documents plan participants can request from their employer — 145
29. Department of Labor audit requests for documentation — 150
30. Future of 401(k) — 157

Prospecting Ideas

1. Two types of corporate retirement plans   1
2. Enhancing the accomplishment of corporate goals with the company 401(k) plan   8
3. A great phrase to memorize and deliver for prospecting   17
4. Vesting schedules and eligibility requirements are a low-cost solution to "shine-up" a 401(k) plan   23
5. Three variables involved in determining how much money we accumulate for our retirement   40
6. Use of testimonial letters #1   41
7. What do you tell people you do?   43
8. Time to upgrade the company 401(k) plan   46
9. Use of vesting schedules to recapture employee contributions   49
10. Listing of lead database vendors   80
11. Surveying local companies   87
12. Keep your eyes open for performance opportunity   91
13. Know whom to contact   92
14. Effective openers   93
15. Goal for the initial contact   95
16. "Hail Mary" when the call is going nowhere   100
17. Use of testimonial letters #2   102
18. Developing match formula comparisons in your territory   106
19. "Crow" when you win   128
20. Stay in touch with plans that you are not chosen to serve   156

Sales Ideas

1. Service will lead to opportunity   12
2. Use the Department of Labor Fee Comparison Worksheet   50
3. Become a search consultant for your 401(k) plan sponsor prospect   50
4. Align yourself with quality service providers   58
5. Use a union "shop" organization when bidding for union 401(k) plans   73
6. Illustration depicting time spent with a prospect to a client   101
7. Prospects ranking concerns for their current plan   104
8. Using an Executive Summary during the sales presentation   110
9. Using Requests For Proposals (RFP)   111
10. Illustrate the potential partnership with the prospect with digital imaging   112
11. Wear a sweatshirt during the sales presentation   117
12. Sample closing statement #1   121
13. Sample closing statement #2   121
14. Effective follow-up ideas   122
15. Supply comparison martixes   125

Service Ideas

1. Local Relationship Manager and Employee Retirement Coach™   5
2. Creative service event promotes 401(k) plan retention and cross-selling   9
   opportunities
3. Cross-selling company management   16
4. Cross-selling other plan participants   16
5. Help trustees to manage their fiduciary responsibilities   28
6. Market volatility presentation   39
7. 401(k) Vendor supplying employee education materials   132
8. Top three reasons employees do not participate in their company 401(k) plan 133
9. Employees have three important decisions to make when they join a 401(k) plan 136
10. Points to reinforce during a market volatility presentation   143
11. Proactive service strategy with plan sponsor clients #1   144
12. Proactive service strategy with plan participants   145
13. Use of promotional dry-marker board at the company   147
14. Proactive service strategy with plan sponsor clients #2   149

Glossary of Terms

401(k) Sales Champion: A financial sales professional who provides focused, value-added service to 401(k) plan sponsors and plan participants to effectively help them accomplish their respective goals.

401(k) Vendor: The financial service company or other organization that provides all or one of the five disciplines of the 401(k) plan.

Active Participants: Current employees who are participating in their employer's retirement plan.

Administrative/Record keeping Fee: The fee for providing record keeping and other 401(k) plan participant administrative services. For start-up or conversion 401(k) plans, these fees typically include charges for processing and communicating information to the plan sponsor, the plan participant, the IRS and DoL.

Annual Audit: Federal law requires that all ERISA covered plans with more than 100 participants be audited by an independent auditor. It is also common to refer to a DoL or IRS examination of a plan as a plan audit.

Annuitization: The process of building recurring commission revenue into your business.

Average Contribution Percentage Test (ACP): Is a required annual test (unless the plan is a safe harbor plan) which examines employer matching contributions and employee after-tax contributions and determines whether the highly compensated employee group is receiving a greater benefit versus the non-highly compensated group.

Average Deferral Percentage Test (ADP): Is a required annual test (unless the plan is a safe harbor plan) which determines whether the highly compensated employee group is contributing to their accounts through 401(k) salary deferrals an allowable amount above limits which are greater than the non-highly compensated employee group is contributing through their own salary deferrals.

Back-End Load: Sales charges due the investment vendor upon the sale or transfer of mutual funds, insurance/annuity products or other investments, which may be reduced and/or eliminated over time.

Balance Forward: An accounting technique by a 401(k) vendor where participant accounts are valued at specific intervals, (monthly or quarterly), and contributions, withdrawals and investment performance are added to the previous participant account balance and forwarded to the end of the present period.

Balance Inquiry Fee: A fee that might be charged each time a participant inquires about their 401(k) account balance.

Bank pooled funds: Money from many different sources, most frequently institutions (pension funds, endowments, foundations, etc.) invested by a bank.

Brokerage Commission: A fee paid to a broker or other intermediary for executing a trade.

Brokerage Window: A 401(k) plan investment choice allowing a plan participant to establish a self-directed brokerage account. (see Self Direction)

Bundled: A 401(k) program structure provided by a 401(k) vendor, where the vendor is supplying all five disciplines for the company 401(k) plan; plan document, plan administration, plan investments, trust services and employee retirement education.

Cash Or Deferred Arrangement (CODA): A qualified retirement plan that allows participants to have a portion of their compensation (otherwise payable in cash) contributed on a pre-tax to a retirement account for their behalf. These arrangements are sometimes referred to as 401(k) arrangements, after section 401(k) of the Internal Revenue Code that allows organizations to sponsor them.

Cliff Vesting: full (100%) vesting in employer contributions after a specified length of service by the plan participant, with no (0%) vesting prior to that time.

Collective Investment Fund: A tax-exempt pooled fund operated by a bank or trust company that commingles the assets of trust accounts for which the bank provides fiduciary services.

Contract Administration Charge: An omnibus charge for costs of administering the insurance/annuity contract prior to the end of a stated time period. The charge typically decreases over time.

Contract Termination Charge: A charge to the 401(k) plan for "surrendering" or "terminating" its insurance/annuity contract prior to the end of a stated time period. The charge typically decreases over time.

Conversion: The process of changing from one (or more) 401(k) vendor(s) to another.

Corporate Trustee: An independent organization which provides oversight responsibility to the plan administration discipline and/or custody of the plan assets for a fee.

Daily Valuation: An accounting technique where participants accounts are valued daily, allowing the plan participant to access current information and effect transactions to their account 24 hours a day, seven days a week.

Defined Benefit Plan: A type of qualified retirement plan in which benefits for an eligible employee are calculated according to a formula or rule, typically based on pay or a negotiated flat-dollar amount and years of service. Contributions are made by the employer and there are usually no employee contributions allowed. The employer bears the risk associated with providing the monetary retirement benefit for the covered employees.

Defined Contribution Plan: A type of qualified plan in which the employer contributes up to a maximum dollar amount for each eligible employee. Employee contributions can also be made. 401(k) plans are a type of defined contribution plan. The amount of retirement benefit received by the eligible employee is based upon the total amount of contributions to their account as well as investment results.

Discovery Meeting: A meeting in which you obtain profiling information with the assistance of the 401(k) plan decision-makers to learn all you can about the company, employees and the current 401(k) program. The information obtained will enhance your ability to acquire the company 401(k) plan.

Distribution Expense: The costs typically associated with processing paperwork and issuing a check for a distribution of plan assets to a participant. May include the generation of IRS Form 1099R. This fee may apply to hardship and other in-service withdrawals as well as to separation-from-service or retirement distributions.

Eligible Employee: Any employee who has achieved the eligibility requirements of age and length of service to the company, allowing them to participate in and receive benefits from the 401(k) plan.

Employee Retirement Income Security Act of 1974: ERISA is the acronym for this legislation which established federal standards for the operation of qualified, employer sponsored retirement plans.

Employee Stock Ownership Plan: ESOP is the acronym for this type of defined contribution plan that provides shares of sponsoring employer stock to participating employees. A leveraged ESOP borrows money to purchase company stock to distribute to employees.

Expense Ratio: The cost of investing and administrating assets, including management fees, in a mutual fund or other collective fund expressed as a percentage of total assets.

Front-end Load: Sales charges due the investment vendor when an investment in a mutual fund, insurance/annuity product or other investment is made.

Individually Managed Account: An investment account managed for a single plan.

Installation Fee: One-time fee for initiating a new 401(k) plan or initiating new services.

Integration: A way to provide a proportionately higher pension benefit or contribution to higher paid employees as a result of taking employer contributions to Social Security into consideration.

Investment Transfer Expense: Fee associated when a plan participant changes their investment allocation, or makes transfers among funding accounts under the plan.

Loan Maintenance and Repayment Tracking Fee: Fee charged to monitor outstanding loans and repayment schedule.

Loan Origination Fee: Fee charged when a plan loan is originally taken out.

Loan Processing Fee: Fee charged to process a loan application.

Management Fee: Fee charged for the management of investments such as collective investment funds, insurance/annuity products, mutual funds and individually managed accounts.

Money Purchase Plan: A type of qualified defined contribution plan which defines mandatory employer contributions to a participant as a fixed percent of the eligible employees pay.

Mortality Risk and Administrative Expense (M&E) Fee: Fee charged by an insurance company to cover the cost of the insurance features of an annuity contract, including the guarantee of a lifetime income payment, interest and expense guarantees, and any death benefit provided during the accumulation period.

Mutual Fund Trailer: An ongoing commission payout to the Financial Professional, usually paid quarterly based on total assets under management within a particular mutual fund.

Negative Enrollment (a.k.a. automatic enrollment): Employees are automatically and immediately enrolled in the company 401(k) plan unless they make a negative election to opt out of the plan. In addition a default savings rate and investment allocation can be pre-determined for the participant.

Nondiscrimination Testing Expense: Tax qualified retirement plans must be administered in compliance with several regulations requiring numerical measurements. The fee charged for the process of determining whether the plan is in compliance is collectively called nondiscrimination testing expense.

Participant Direction: The ability of the plan participant to invest their account balance among the investment choices in the 401(k) plan.

Participant Education Materials/Distribution Expenses: All costs (including travel expense) associated with providing print, video, software and/or live instruction to educate employees about how the 401(k) plan works, the plan investment funds available and asset allocation strategies. There may be a one-time cost associated with implementing a new 401(k) plan, as well as ongoing costs for an existing plan.

Plan Administration: The accounting discipline of the 401(k) where plan participant account balances and all plan activity are reported.

Plan Assets: The contributions by the plan participants and the employer along with any gains or minus any loses sustained.

Plan Document: A legal contract which once completed and adopted by the plan sponsor establishes the 401(k) plan.

Plan Document Determination Letter Fee (Filing Fee): Fee associated with preparing and filing IRS required documentation, including the request for a determination letter (document issued by the IRS stating whether the plan meets the qualifications for tax-advantaged treatment).

Plan Loan: The tax laws allow 401(k) plan participants to borrow from their accounts up to prescribed limits. This is an optional plan feature.

Plan Participant: Any eligible employee who has an account balance in the 401(k) plan.

Plan Sponsor: The employer who adopts and maintains the 401(k) plan for the employees of the company.

Plan Sponsor Book (PSB): A tool prepared by a 401(k) Sales Champion™ to assist the plan sponsor in the management of their fiduciary responsibilities, namely investment management selection and monitoring, as well as employee retirement education events.

Product Termination Fee: Investment-product charges associated with terminating one or all of a 401(k) vendor's investment products.

Profit Sharing Plan: A type of qualified defined contribution plan which allows discretionary employer contributions to a participant as a percent of the eligible employees pay. A 401(k) is typically an addition to a profit sharing plan.

QDRO (Qualified Domestic Relations Order): A judgment, decree or order that creates or recognizes an alternate payee's (such as a former spouse, child, etc.) right to receive all or a portion of a plan participant's retirement plan benefits.

Regulation 404(c): In order to be in compliance with this voluntary DoL regulation, a company should offer plan participants at least three core investment alternatives, each of which offers a diversified and substantially different risk and return characteristics from the others. The selections offered must provide opportunity for the plan participants to substantially minimize the risk of large loses, while still maintaining their ability to materially affect the potential return on the invested areas. The three investments used to satisfy the broad-range requirement must have investment change dates at least quarterly. Participants must be given sufficient information to make informed investment decisions.

Request For Proposal (RFP): A written document which contains questions developed by the plan sponsor or search consultant. Candidate financial sales professionals and the 401(k) vendor(s) answer the RFP. The answers to the questions help the plan sponsor to narrow and select the company 401(k) plan service provider(s).

Retirement Coach™: A role performed by a 401(k) Sales Champion™ to empower plan participants to confidently use their company 401(k) plan to accumulate and manage their retirement wealth.

Self Direction: The ability of a plan participant to utilize a Brokerage Window to manage their account and purchase any security allowed by law and available through the brokerage firm.

Separate Account: An asset account established by a life insurance company, separate from other funds of the life insurance company, offering investment funding options for retirement plans.

Service Provider Termination Charge: Plan administration costs associated with terminating a relationship with a 401(k) vendor, with the permanent termination of the plan, or with the termination of specific plan services. These may be termed "surrender" or "transfer" charges.

Signature Ready 5500: A form which all qualified retirement plans must file annually with the IRS.

Start-up/Enrollment Expense: Costs associated with providing materials to educate employees about the 401(k) plan, and enrolling employees in the plan. This may be part of, or included in, the education programs. There may be one-time costs associated with implementing a new plan, as well as ongoing enrollment costs.

Third Party Administrator (TPA): An organization which provides plan administration services such as plan participant record keeping, compliance testing and reporting services.

Trustee Direction: Plan assets invested by the plan trustees on behalf of the plan participants.

Vesting: The process in a qualified defined benefit or defined contribution plan where the participating employee earns a non-forfeitable right to a percent of employer contributions. Once an employee is fully vested, they are 100% owner in the amount of past, current and future employer contributions to their account. Participating employees are always 100% vested in the amount of their own contributions that they make to their retirement account, such as those made through a 401(k) plan.

Voice Response Unit (VRU): "800" number service providing participants 24 hour, 7 day a week access to their account information. Also know as a Voice Response Service (VRS).

Unbundled: Where two or more 401(k) vendors provide the five disciplines to the company 401(k) plan: plan document, plan administration, plan investments, trust services and employee retirement education.

Wrap Fee: An inclusive fee generally based on the percentage of assets in an investment program, which typically provides asset allocation, execution of transactions and other administrative services.

Written Investment Policy: A document put in place by the plan sponsor to help the trustees to select and monitor the plans' investment choices.

RESOURCE SECTION

Books: Technical Information

Qualified Plans I: Plan Types and Benefits
www.dearborn.com
800-252-0866

Qaulified Plans II: Qualification and Design
www.dearborn.com
800-252-0866

401(k) Plans
www.dearborn.com
800-252-0866

The Pension Answer Book
www.aspenpub.com
800-638-8467

ERISA Fiduciary Answer Book
www.aspenpub.com
800-638-8467

10 Minute Guide to 401(k) Plans
www.mcp.com
800-716-0044

The Complete Idiot's Guide to 401(k) Plans
www.mcp.com
800-716-0044

401(k) Today: Designing, Maintaining and Maximizing Your Company's Plan
www.bkconnection.com
800-929-2929

401(k) Plan Handbook for Sponsors
www.phdirect.com
800-947-7700

Financial Sales Professionals: Marketing / Sales

www.knowhow401k.com	KnowHow 401(k)
www.401konnect.com	401Konnect.com, Inc.
www.advisormarketing.com	AdvisorMarketing.com, Inc.
www.onwallstreet.com	On Wall Street Magazine
www.rrmag.com	Registered Representative Magazine
www.retirementsuite.com	RetirementSuite.com, Inc.
www.search401k.com	Search401k.com, Inc.
www.ticker.com	Ticker Magazine
www.401kexchange.com	Where Plan Buyers and Sellers Meet

Financial Sales Professionals: Technical and Industry Information

www.401khelpcenter.com	401(k) Help Center
www.amercoll.edu	The American College
www.asec.org	American Savings Education Council
www.bog.frb.fed.us	Board of Governors of the Federal Reserve System
www.stats.bls.gov	Bureau of Labor Statistics
www.cfp-board.org	Certified Financial Planner Board of Standards
www.cfonet.com	CFO Magazine
www.yardeni.com	Dr. Ed Yardeni Economics Network
www.benefitslink.com	Employee Benefits Compliance and Information
www.ebri.org	Employee Benefit Research Institute
www.employer-employee.com	Employer and Employee relations
www.ioma.com	Institute of Management & Administration
www.irs.ustreas.gov	Internal Revenue Service
www.ici.org	Investment Company Institute
www.imca.org	Investment Management Consultants Association
www.investment news.com	Investment News
www.naip.com	National Association of Investment Professionals
www.nasdr.com	National Association of Securities Dealers
www.nasd.com	National Association of Securities Dealers
www.nasaa.org	North American Securities Administators Association
www.pionline.com	Pension and Investments Magazine
www.dol.gov/dol/pwba	Pension and Welfare Benefits Administration
www.plansponsor.com	Plan Sponsor Magazine
www.psca.org	Profit Sharing / 401(k) Council of America
www.entreworld.org	Resources for Entrepreneurs
www.sec.gov	Securities and Exchange Commission
www.sia.com	Securities Industry Association
www.ssa.gov	Social Security Administration
www.asclu.org	Society of Financial Service Professionals™
www.uschamber.org	United States Chamber of Commerce
www.ustreas.gov	The United States Treasury
www.cyberinvest.com	Links to websites

Lead Database Vendors

www.pensionplanet.com	Dunn and Bradstreet / Pension Planet Database
www.freeerisa.com	FreeERISA, Inc.
www.judydiamond.com	Judy Diamond Database
www.larkspurdata.com	Larkspur Data
www.mobiusg.com	Mobius Group
www.mmdaccess.com	Money Market Directory

General

www.inter800.com	Internet 800 Toll Free Directory

Plan Participants

www.timyounkin.com	401(k) Advocate
www.aaii.com	American Association of Individual Investors
www.aarp.org	American Association of Retired Persons
www.amex.com	The American Stock Exchange
www.freeerisa.com	Answers To Plan Participant Questions
www.401kafe.com	Community Resource for 401(k) Plan Participants
www.consumerfed.org	Consumer Federation of America
www.pueblo.gsa.gov	Consumer Information Center
www.cyberinvest.com	CyberInvest: links to additional sites
www.financialengines.com	Financial Engines
www.jumpstartcoalition.org	Jump$tart Coalition for Personal Financial Literacy
www.401kforum.com	M-Power
www.money.com	Money Magazine
www.morningstar.com	Morningstar
www.nasdaq.com	NASDAQ
www.nyse.com	The New York Stock Exchange
www.familyhaven.com	Resources for the Entire Family
www.smartmoney.com	SmartMoney Magazine
www.investorwords.com	defines >4000 investment term